CAM

The Mountai

A PRACTICAL (

A.J.Drake
4th Edition 1995

CONTENTS

Copyright   A.J.Drake   ISBN 0 9509580 3 4

PREFACE TO THE FOURTH EDITION

Once more the revision work for a new edition has taken much longer than expected and regrettably there has been a year with the book being out of print. Judging by the demand since summer 1994, Cambrian Way has become more established as *the* mountain walk to do and it was gratifying to find "Strider", the journal of the Long Distance Walkers' Association, calling it the "best buy" for a mountain walk in Britain.

The Cambrian Way provides an excuse to visit most of the best parts of Wales and since the last edition was published I have spent over 160 days on or near the Way and in particular I have walked the whole of it in a series of week long sessions over three years, plus a weekend, with friends from the Offa's Dyke Association. This enabled many improvements to the strip maps to be made, and not least of the value of the exercise was proving that one can go wrong on routes one thought one knew well, but which are altogether more difficult in cloud. The hazard of the final stretch across the Carneddau, and its danger to those who have no spare days at the end of a holiday, was amply proved when a gale that one could not stand up in resulted in a retreat, and a return next year to complete the Way.

The changes from the previous edition are extensive. Apart from many alterations to the maps the whole text has been put on computer, which has enabled many more changes to be made than was convenient with the typewriter generated text before. Hopefully I will get into computer map making by the time of the next edition. The accommodation list continues to be the biggest headache and is almost impossible to keep up to date. I believe in personal contact at intervals rather than annual checks, and stay overnight at most establishments at least once. For the currency of at least this edition I intend to provide an updated accommodation list on receipt of 50p in stamps and a stamped addressed envelope.

There has been criticism of certain guidebook writers who have not perhaps done their research into rights of way and access too thoroughly, and whose guidebooks never get revised. There have been arguments about revisions to the late Arthur Wainwright's superb guides to the Lake District and to his Coast to Coast Walk in particular. There are parallels between the latter and Cambrian Way in that they are both coast to coast routes without official recognition, but what I lack in artistic ability I hope I have made up for by keeping the guide reasonably up to date. and free from access problems.

Welsh rights of way are still generally in a parlous state,with little progress being made towards the government target of the network being put in order by the turn of the century. The Countryside Council for Wales has had its funding savaged cut so that grant aiding the rural counties of Wales to deal with rights of way problems is unlikely to happen and getting the few problems on Cambrian Way solved will still be difficult and frustrating. On the access front there is an interesting experiment in some parts of Wales, called Tir Cymen (see page 15), such that the amount of Cambrian Way on open access land without any known access arrangements is now only 1.8% of the whole route.

A welcome recent development which will hopefully deal with some of the more intractable erosion problems is the formation of the British Upland Footpath Trust. The enjoyment of reaching the principal summits of Wales will perhaps some day be less marred by erosion scars, thanks to generous donations to the trust

Tony Drake

June 1995.

THE MOUNTAIN CONNOISSEUR'S WALK

The Cambrian Way is a mountain walking route from Cardiff to Conwy traversing much of the highest, wildest and most scenically beautiful parts of Wales. It was originally conceived as a long distance path to be created under the National Parks & Access to the Countryside Act 1949, but following much opposition the Countryside Commission abandoned the scheme for its creation in 1982. The Way described in this guidebook is basically the route originally proposed by the Cambrian Way Committee in 1971, with some modifications to make greater use of existing public rights of way. Where the public does not have a legal or permissive right to go the Way is across mountain and moorland on routes where there has been de facto access for many years.

The Cambrian Way is designed for the connoisseur of mountain walking. It is not intended to appeal to the "beeliner" and those of the John o' Groats to Land's End by road mentality. It is for those who like to follow a well tried route, where the quality of the scenery has been the first consideration in planning. The Cambrian Way should be walked only for the pleasure and achievement it brings to the individual. It is not for the masochists who need to be spurred on by sponsorship.

At 274 miles (440Km) the length of the Cambrian Way is 24 miles more than the Pennine Way. A possible schedule making maximum use of youth hostels would be 293 miles. The ascent involved is 61,540 feet (18,742 metres) which is nearly double that of the Pennine Way. This greater ascent must be very seriously taken into account not only as to the length of time required, but also as to whether the Way should be attempted at all, especially if backpacking. With the average time taken for the Pennine Way being about nineteen days, the Cambrian Way is likely to need at least three days more. It is much more of a mountaineering expedition than the Pennine Way and is more of a high level route than the West Highland Way. 64% of the route is at over 800 feet (240 metres) above sea level. 20% is over 2,000 feet (610m) and 2% is over 3,000 feet (915m).

A Countryside Commission survey of 1972 identified two factors above all others as to why people walked the Pennine Way. These were the scenery and the challenge. The Cambrian Way has both scenery and challenge in abundance.

Almost all of Wales can be said to be attractive but those parts designated as national parks have been selected because they are extensive tracts of country where their natural beauty calls for preservation and enhancement for the purpose of promoting their enjoyment by the public. 60% of the Cambrian Way is through the national parks of Snowdonia and the Brecon Beacons. A further 20% in central Wales is through what the Countryside Commission considered worthy of national park status but which the Secretary of State for Wales rejected as such in 1973. Even the remaining 20% is mostly through pleasant rolling country. Little industrialisation is seen and only one motorway is crossed. The biggest eyesore is probably Trawsfynydd nuclear power station.

The challenge is to find the physical and mental stamina to walk the continuous route. The Cambrian Way should not be the first long distance walk to be undertaken. Shorter, less arduous, ways should be tried first. Additional attributes are required on Cambrian Way. Wind and rain at higher altitudes can be quite destructive and demoralising. Waterproof clothing is absolutely essential and walkers should be warned of the really lethal effect of hypothermia. caused by the combination of a wet body and the cold conditions frequently experienced in mountains. Although much of the Way is on popular routes, most of it is unfrequented and where the way is undefined on the ground and is unwaymarked. The additional height means that much of the time will be in cloud where navigation is bound to be difficult. Ability to use a compass is essential but more important is being able to read maps and particularly to interpret contours. The maps in this guidebook are designed so that they provide complete navigation requirements together with the 1 : 50,000 Landranger maps of the Ordnance Survey . The size of the guide is just less than the folded size of the Landranger maps to facilitate either carrying in a long hip pocket of one's walking breeches or, mounted in the open position, back to back with two side by side segments of the OS. map in a map case or transparent plastic bag .

The routes described are not the result of just walking over the ground once and writing it up. Much surveying of possible routes was carried out by members of the Cambrian Way Committee, and the author must have spent several hundred days in surveys. The legal status of the route traversed has been carefully checked and visits have been made to all the county councils involved to view public path definitive maps, road records and commons registers. A few obstruction problems have been reported to the highway authorities. The original proposals assumed that some new rights of way would be created following approval of the route by the Secretary of State for Wales. Surprisingly the greater use of rights of way has only resulted in an increase of six miles (2%) over the length proposed in 1971. As will be seen in the analysis on a later page, 87½ % of the Way is where the public either has a right to go or where there is permissive use. 10% is over rural commons and the remaining 2½ % is over mountain, moorland and paths where de facto access has been enjoyed for many years.

It must be stressed that there is no official recognition to the Cambrian Way, either by the Countryside Council for Wales (successors to the Countryside Commission) or any of the authorities. Whilst the Commission strongly supported the project until 1978, most of the county and district councils along the route and the two national park authorities were opposed to the concept. The farming unions were vociferous in their opposition. Hopefully the use of the Way resulting from this guide will prove that the opposition was unjustified and that it will become accepted as has Wainwright's popular Coast to Coast walk across northern England, though without some of the problems caused by lack of adequate research into rights of way and access land status, and failure to update, that characterised that particular walk.

Most of the well known summits of Wales are included, with Snowdon the highest point in England and Wales as a fitting climax. Some lesser known summits are visited but some of the well known ones are omitted. Notable amongst these are the Arans, not omitted because of the access problems that arose there but because a route over the Arans does not fit in conveniently with the more interesting traverse of Cader Idris and the Rhinogs. The route is not always on the tops and sometimes deliberately follows a valley where the valley is particularly attractive. Thus the wild Doethie valley is followed for several miles and descent is made at Devil's Bridge to the gorge of the Rheiddol. Wales has many attractive woodlands of traditional hardwoods and several of these are visited.

Planning overnight accommodation is the biggest headache for most who walk long distance paths. The backpacker has fewer problems but must still find a site where his or her night's stay will not cause offence. Those prepared to hostel will find the Youth Hostel chain is already more complete than it was on the Pennine Way when that path was opened, even though several have closed since the Cambrian Way project was mooted. Those wanting a little more luxury will find the bed and breakfast houses provide the traditonal Welsh "welcome in the hillside" and that there is an adequate selection in the comprehensive list in this guide

THE HISTORY OF THE CAMBRIAN WAY

My first involvement in long distance path planning was in the early 1950s when the Ramblers Association in Gloucestershire did the initial planning for the Cotswold Way. About the same time I was involved in negotiations for amendments to the designated route for the Offa's Dyke path in the Wye Valley. Between 1957 and 1960 I was involved in the planning of a serial walk along the Dyke path for the three Gloucestershire rambling clubs. These were very popular and when it was over the cry was "What can we do next? " I did some preliminary planning for a route from Gloucester to Snowdon via the Black Mountains, Brecon Beacons and Plynlimon. The enormous attraction of this mostly mountain route was apparent, but the Gloucetsreshire ramblers did not take it up. It was not until 1967 that it occurred to me to wonder why no one had proposed a long distance route over the principal mountains of Wales. Soundings in R.A. and Y.H.A. circles in Wales brought an immediate and enthusiastic response . S.Wales Area of the R.A. and S.Wales Region of the Y.H.A. each successfully put up motions to their respective national councils in March 1968 calling for the creation of a Cambrian Way Long Distance Footpath.

The Cambrian Way Committee . Roger Brickell, the South Wales R.A. secretary at that time, convened a meeting at Kington Youth Hostel on June 23rd 1968, at which a Cambrian Way Committee was formed with myself as chairman and Roger as secretary. A predominantly high level mountain route was to be surveyed and various organisations undertook sections by counties. The south part was divided between the R.A., Y.H.A., the Brecon Beacons Voluntary Wardens Association and Pontypool Group of the R.A. In the north the British Mountaineering Council was to be offered the Caernarvonshire section but turned out to be hostile to the whole concept . Subsequently the R.A. and Y.H.A., based on Liverpool, joined forces, led by Bill Hall and Brian Steventon respectively, and surveyed all the northern half.

The survey methods varied considerably. In the south some of the committee, notably Bob Rowson and Keith Mascetti were already knowledgeable of their area. Denis Veasey, David Robinson and Don Sutor made surveys in the lesser known Elenydd and concluded that the western side of that wild area had fewer forestry problems. The Liverpool ramblers and hostellers had different methods and descended on their allotted area by coach and dispersed into several survey groups. Although I had visited much of Wales, particularly on meets of the Gloucestershire Mountaineering Club, my roving commission on all sections took me to many delightful parts of Wales I might never have gone to.

My first proposal was for a route from Capel-y-ffin to Snowdon but this soon got extended in both directions. Capel-y-ffin was clearly no equivalent of Edale on the Pennine Way but proposals to start a little further south at Abergavenny did not satisfy the South Wales members of the committee, who devised a route from Cardiff skirting the coalfield. At the north end the natural extension was to the North Wales coast and soon the attraction of the long ridge of the Carneddau and the idea of a castle to castle route clinched Conwy as the northern terminal.

At the subsequent three meetings of the committee the difficulty of arriving at a consensus view increased and there was a temptation to suggest alternatives because of disagreement. However, certain alternatives were agreed upon for safety reasons, such as a lower level alternative to the Rhinog ridgeline, and the Pyg Track or Crib Goch on Snowdon .

One alternative never properly resolved was whether to go north from Plynlimon to Cader Idris via Machynlleth or the longer way via Dylife, Dinas Mawddwy and Maesglase. (See later in the guide for the main arguments.) There was considerable discussion over the Black Mountains, partly as to whether to include them, and, if so, where to cross over to the Brecon Beacons. I never liked the variation proposed via Mynydd Llangorse and Talybont, because it omitted the very fine Pen Allt Mawr ridge, and the Llangattock cave area. The Brecon Park wardens advocated use of the Brecon and Usk canal towpath from Llangattock and Talybont but I could never see keen mountain walkers wanting to walk nine miles of towpath however attractive.

The 1971 Proposals. On July 10th 1971, after the ceremony at Knighton declaring the Offa's Dyke Path officially open, I handed John Cripps, chairman of the Countryside Commission, a set of maps giving the Cambrian Way Committee's proposed route for Cambrian Way. In November that year I produced what I called the **Interim Report** and this lamentably was the only information on the Cambrian Way that I found time to produce until the first edition of this guidebook in 1984. Many hundreds of a scruffy 34 page duplicated report were sold to would be walkers until most of the stencils wore out.

The Countryside Commission had the responsibility for making recommendations to the Secretaries of State for the Environment or for Wales for the creation of long distance paths, under provisions of the National Parks & Access to the Countryside Act 1949.(Since 1991 these duties have been taken over by the **Countryside Council for Wales)** Routes approved by the Secretary of State become the responsibility of the local authorities to create with 100% grant from national funds. New rights of way can be created by agreement or compulsorily by creation order. The Commission from the beginning made encouraging noises and first mentioned the Cambrian Way in its annual report for 1968. The Interim Report was well received but it was made clear that restricted resources would dictate only limited commitment to the proposals. This proved to be a considerable understatement, such that the Commission's next four annual reports only indicated that the route was " under consideration". It sought to get reactions from the likely user organisations before approaching local authority and landowning interests. The Committee for Wales of the Countryside Commission was enthusiastic both under the chairmanship of Dr. Margaret Davies and later of Trevor Lewis and James Kegie.

In April 1976 the Commission approved the Cambrian Way project in principle and in September 1977 started official consultations on the basis of a map showing both the Cambrian Way Committee's route and the Commission's **Preferred Route** which differed in many respects . All the principal summits in Snowdonia were omitted. The route was to go over the Arans and the Arenigs instead of the Rhinogs and Cader Idris. The crossover from Black Mountains to Brecon Beacons was to be via Mynydd Llangorse.

Following opposition from many quarters, the Commission issued another line in January 1980 called a **Consultation Route**. This time the Cambrian Way Committee's route was not shown on the map, though the new route was closer to it than the 1977 line. Snowdon was included but still not the ridge of the Carneddau. Cader Idris was included and a route to the seaward side of the Rhinogs instead of a route over the Arans, where in the meantime an access row had blown up. The Black Mountains were omitted altogether following pressure from the national park - authority .

There had been much criticism of lack of consultation by the Commission, so to meet this it had decided to appoint **field officers** to meet landowners and other authorities. The first field officer, John Tetlow, a lecturer of the Department of Town Planning at the University of Wales, was appointed for a year and asked to report on the southern section up to Llandovery. He started off full of enthusiasm and the right ideas but when confronted with the opposition of commoners' committees and the national park authority, came up with some extraordinary compromises. Neither Pen y Fan nor the Carmarthen Van summits were to be part of the route, Pen y Fan because of erosion problems on the obvious route, and the Vans because the commoners would only agree to a route creeping round the base of the common and through conifer woods. The Cnewr Estate would not agree to any access during its lambing period (April 15th to May 10th) and the Countryside Commission was not prepared to have a long distance path with such a limitation.

The second field officer to be appointed, Donald Hoare, of Cwmystwyth, a former principal of an outdoor pursuits centre in Wales, fared better than John Tetlow and found general acceptance of the Cambrian Way proposals in the central section.

After years of support for the project and considerable determination to see the Cambrian Way designated, the Countryside Commission suddenly caved in and, with regret, abandoned it in January 1982. It concluded that there was continuing and widespread opposition to the proposed route, even when alternatives were considered. It was one of the earliest major decisions of the Commission following the appointment of Derek (later Sir Derek) Barber as its new chairman and who was advised to abandon the project by Martin Fitton, then the Principal Welsh Officer of the Commission, and currently National Park Officer for the Brecon Beacons. The decision was seen as an act of appeasement to the Welsh farmers in the hope of more cooperation on other countryside issues.

Donald Hoare's contract was terminated and the Commission never got round to appointing a field officer for the northern section. Who knows what ghastly compromises he or she might have been forced into in the Snowdonia National Park?

The Recreational Organisations

The Ramblers Association has consistently supported the Cambrian Way concept. Its National Executive Committee approved the principle of a Cambrian Way following a meeting, which I attended, in July 1972 but agreed that any guide on the subject should stress that it was a mountain route . It was proposed that the title should be "The Cambrian Mountain Way". In the late 80s support for the Cambrian Way was confirmed as the RA's preferred additional national trail in Wales.

The **Youth Hostels Association** likewise consistently supported the idea of a high level route with low level alternatives. It looked forward to an exciting new outlet for the energies of young travellers.

The **British Mountaineering Council's** North Wales Committee was bitterly opposed to the idea of a Cambrian Way and in particular to it going over the Rhinogs. At a meeting in February 1972, at which I was representing the Gloucestershire Mountaineering Club, only the London Mountaineering Club representative gave support. The B.M.C.'s South-west and Southern Committee, covering South Wales, decided in favour so that the matter was called in nationally. I attended a meeting of the Committee of Management in October 1972 and after an hour and a half's debate Cambrian Way was approved by II votes to 4 . Subsequently however the B.M.C. Safety Committee secured a reversal of the decision on safety grounds, and thought that designation would "encourage peak baggers and merit badge enthusiasts into difficult and remote areas". The North Wales Committee was asked to work out an alternative to the Rhinogs and it was their route over the relatively dull Arenig Fawr and moorland to the south-east of Ffestiniog that appeared as part of the Countryside Commission's preferred route in 1977.

The County Councils and the National Parks

Numerically the county councils were equally divided as to the merits of a Cambrian Way, Gwent, South Glamorgan and Mid Glamorgan being in favour with Dyfed, Gwynedd and Powys against. Those against however controlled 87% of the proposed route.

Both the national park authorities opposed the Cambrian Way. **Brecon Beacons National Park** claimed that the route proposed was neither logical nor in keeping with the policies of the national park plan. That plan defined the Carmarthen Vans as a remote and vulnerable area where additional recreation activity would not be encouraged by the provision of further facilities. The use of two further ridges of the Black Mountains for a long distance path was said to be difficult to accept and support. Despite the 100% grants available for long distance paths it was argued that concentration of limited resources on long distance paths reduced the amount of work carried out on the path network generally. It was pointed out that the cost of erosion work in the Brecon Beacons was falling entirely on the national park and the National Trust, but no mention was made that 100% grant could be available if the erosion was on an official long distance route.

The opposition continued and the national park committee even went to the length of passing a resolution in 1986 to ban the sales of this book from its Mountain Centre near Brecon.

Snowdonia National Park in its national park plan (1977) said "The National Park Authority is not convinced of the desirability of the proposed Cambrian Way long distance footpath. In particular they are opposed to the suggested route linking most of the principal summits of Snowdonia. The Authority will therefore seek further discussions on the topic with the Countryside Commission and other interested bodies. " They certainly had discussions with the Commission but not with the R.A. or Y.H.A.

The Farming Interests

Both the **National Farmers Union** and the **Farmers Union of Wales** were vociferous in their opposition to Cambrian Way and used their powerful lobby to influence the local authorities and park committees. The **Country Landowners Association** was apparently not opposed to the project.

THE INSTANT CAMBRIAN WAY

The arguments raged furiously from 1968 to 1982 as to whether a Cambrian Way was desirable and if so where it should go. If the project had not been abandoned, the arguments would probably have gone on for decades and the end result, if any, would at best have been a set of miserable compromises.

It was becoming apparent, even before abandonment, that if the compromises being considered were adopted, there would have arisen the anomalous situation of Cambrian Way walkers watching others go the obvious well established ways while they were plodding round the edges of commons and missing the tops. Guidebooks would have appeared advocating different routes to the official line and the whole concept of long distance paths would have fallen into disrepute.

Following abandonment there was a freedom to choose any way over which the public has a right of way or access, or where there is permissive use. On commons and other open country it is reasonable to describe well used routes - there would have been no books on mountain walks in Wales if rights of way only had to be followed.

With hindsight it is perhaps a pity I did not produce a guidebook during the mid 70s but the need not to prejudice possible new rights of way was felt to be paramount. After abandonment much further survey was carried out to make more use of existing rights of way. In the event I was "pipped at the post" by Richard Sale, whose "A Cambrian Way" was published in February 1984. Constables had commissioned Richard to write a book which was not to be published until the route became official. After abandonment they decided to go ahead but to avoid certain controversial areas . Subtitled " A personal guide to an unofficial route", the book is not a practical guide and handbook as this book sets out to be, but has 270 pages packed with fascinating reading, mostly historical, and which makes excellent reading after a day on the Cambrian Way. Richard and I had several meetings to coordinate routes but we agreed to differ on some. Richard's book was published too early to take advantage of the purchase of part of Fforest Fawr by Brecon Beacons National Park and the permissive arrangements for the Cnewr estate had not been announced. Although Richard uses the Machynlleth variant from Plynlimon, he did write up the Dinas Mawddwy route as an alternative, but Constables thought the book was long enough. Hopefully others will write books on other aspects of the Cambrian Way such as the industrial archaeology, geology and bird life.

How can it be that the Cambrian Way, officially abandoned after much opposition, suddenly came into existence at the behest of Messrs. Drake and Sale? Is it irresponsible to take advantage of the right of any citizen to suggest to others where they may walk? Some books have undoubtedly caused embarrassment where insufficient research has been carried out as to rights of way and as to possible impacts on wildlife and erosion problems. The public status of the routes in this guidebook has been the subject of all reasonable checks and has been made by one who has a background of 44 years experience in handling rights of way problems. The sections of the route over de facto access land on rural commons (10%) and other mountain and moorland (2½ %) have been carefully chosen to be along well established routes where even the most law abiding walker would not feel it necessary to try to ascertain who the owner was and to ask permission to use.

The following pages detail how the aspects that caused opposition have been considered and taken into account in evolving the routes in this guide. Meanwhile it is pertinent to ask how different the walker will find the route compared with the official long distance paths.

Some sections are already popular routes and are maintained to a reasonable standard, but many sections, including some in the national parks, are poorly maintained or not at all, so walkers must take things as they find them. One of the joys of Cambrian Way is that on many of the higher level sections the way is undefined on the ground. Some of these sections may develop a defined path in time but much will still be wild and give that sense of remoteness that so many seek and do not find on our long distance paths.

The main difference that long distance path addicts will find is that there is little signposting and even less waymarking than one may be accustomed to. Stiles and gates are generally of a low standard. These aspects are elaborated on below. Several obstructions have been found and reported to the county councils, with varying results. Enforcement procedures are none existent or painfully slow and weak in most parts of Wales. Some of the problems reported have taken years to resolve and are difficult to follow up adequately at a distance. In some instances diversions are desirable to provide a better route, but take a long time to process, as notably the diversion at Dinas Mawddwy which took 11 years. Two diversions in Forestry Enterprise land, stimulated by the author, have legalised obstructions made in the 1960s.

There are about 90 stiles and 165 gates on the main route - a fair number but compared to the Offa's Dyke Path, with its 450 stiles and 125 gates (in only 176 miles), Cambrian Way is clearly less of a steeplechase. The difference reflects how different the terrain and land use is, with so much more open country. However, that said, be warned about the gates. Very few Welsh gates are properly hung. The majority are held up at one or both ends with binder twine and sometimes with barbed wire. Getting over these gates can be a greater hazard than many more expected dangers. Maintenance of stiles and gates is the responsibility of whoever maintains the fence, wall or hedge. A grant of at least 25% of the cost is available but seldom claimed as it is just not worth the bother. One might expect gates in regular use to be reasonably well maintained but little used gates, and more particularly stiles, are way down most farmers' priority list for attention. There is little incentive to improve stiles and gates for the benefit of the public and often a distinct inclination to discourage passage by those whose dogs may chase sheep.The bonanza of schemes in the late 80s, using unemployed labour, that got so much work done on footpaths in England never got going in the remoter Welsh counties. Voluntary work is relatively undeveloped but is increasing.

As with maintenance, so also the extent of signposting and waymarking is patchy. More waymarking is desirable to avoid trespass in the lower sections, in the interests of both walker and farmer. I have waymarked several sections, mostly in Forestry Enterprise land, using the Countryside Commission system of yellow painted arrows for footpaths and blue for bridleways. (plus usually the Welsh hat logo at beginning of each section) I am willing to waymark other stretches by agreement with the farmer concerned. On the open mountains waymarking is much less acceptable and appropriate. Cairns are the natural and traditional method, though less efficient than arrows, but should be used sparingly, such as at particular descent points such as the top of the Zig Zags on Snowdon.

MEETING THE OPPOSITION

This section reviews the main reasons for opposition to the designation of the Cambrian Way as an official long distance path and shows how these aspects have been taken into account in planning the routes in this guide.

Erosion

It is only in the last thirty years that erosion has been taken seriously. The enormous increase in mountain walking since the second world war caused the breaking up of the surface of many popular routes. While natural erosion is accepted as a fact of life erosion that is man made offends. Attitudes to erosion are now less hysterical than they were when Cambrian Way was first advocated and research and experiment has shown that much erosion can be coped with or prevented, though at considerable cost. Other more difficult problems remain and seem insoluble. One is inclined to feel that if we can land men on the moon then surely something can be done about erosion. It should not be necessary to discourage access to mountains because what amounts to a very small area is wearing away offensively and because some of such problems defy solution. Like the Cambrian Way itself, erosion is a challenge to be tackled and not something that is used as an excuse to discourage whorthwhile activities.

A sense of proportion is necessary in considering erosion. A few thousand extra walkers going up Snowdon will make little difference when the numbers using the paths there run into millions over the years. Where excessive numbers have caused erosion remedial action appropriate to the situation is a justifiable expense. The public had the Snowdon paths on the cheap in the past, but under the management scheme of recent years sterling work has been done by both volunteers and paid staff and the problem is now under control.

Much consideration has been given to erosion problems in planning the Cambrian Way route in this guide. As the Cambrian Way is envisaged as a south to north route and since most erosion is caused in descent, (and more particularly by those who run down), many eroded spots which are taken in ascent are not likely to be further eroded by Cambrian Way traffic. Where the eroded ascent is itself a hazard, such as Penyrole-wen, an alternative, albeit longer, ascent has been recommended. Some eroded descents have been avoided such as the north face of Blorenge and the descent from Glyder Fawr to Llyn Cwn and Cwm Idwal .

One type of erosion which is never likely to be a serious problem on the Cambrian Way, but which has often been quoted against it, is the traverse of peat bogs of the kind which cause such problems on the Pennine Way. The dropping of enormous slabs by helicopter, which is the latest attempt to solve the Pennine Way peatbog problem, will not be necessary on the Cambrian Way.

Horse riding has been the main cause of erosion on the Black Mountains but it would be most unfair to deny walkers the superb mountain walking there because horse riding had not been adequately brought under control.

Many sections are on broad ridges where, if use had been spread evenly, no breaking up of the grass cover would have occurred. Inevitably however people tend to follow where a path becomes visible, and if used to excess erosion occurs. Our Mountain Connoisseur must use discretion and decide whether to walk well away from the worn path or whether using the path will cause no more erosion. Generally one can serve the cause better by keeping to one side, but not immediately on the edge of the path - that's the next bit to go.

The relative contribution of Cambrian Way walkers to erosion at already eroded sites will be small but care has had to be taken in planning to avoid routes where only a relatively little usage could cause a nasty gash in the mountainside. For this reason steep descents have been avoided such as the new permissive way off Fan Gihirych on the Cnewr Estate.

The ghastly upper section of the Watkin Path was included in the Countryside Commission's 1980 consultative route yet this part of the Snowdon Horseshoe is quite unnecessary if approaching Snowdon from the south-east. The much nicer Allt Maenderyn ridge leading to Bwlch Main is also showing some signs of having appeared in guide books, but it is a wide stony ridge which is unlikely to provide serious problems and will not wear away for a few million years yet.

An unsolved problem is the south-east ridge of Pen y Fan which is a much softer slope. Any solution is likely to look artificial. Probably large stone steps are the answer but unfortunately they are not so readily available as they were for repair of the Snowdon paths.

At the time of editing the 4th edition a newly formed body,the *British Uplands Footpaths Trust,* supported by mountaineering and rambling interests together with camping and outdoor leisure trade interests had been formed to raise money for sensitive repair of eroded popular upland footpaths. Hopefully some of the money raised will ensure remedial action on some of Cambrian Way's intractable erosion problems

The Farmers

I am sure the farmers were needlessly alarmed about the Cambrian Way. They tend to see any proposals for more public access as meaning more sheep worried and killed by dogs, more gates left open, more walls and fences climbed over and more vandalism generally. Each farmer you meet has some horrific tale to tell. One bad incident is inclined to sour a farmer for ever against the public.

Some farmers are very possessive, while others have a greater sense of holding the land in trust and are willing to share use with those who get a pleasure from walking the mountains. Most Welsh farmers are friendly and enjoy a chat if they are not too busy. In all my walks planning the Cambrian Way I have only once been challenged by a farmer and that was on a right of way.

The farmers are a very powerful lobby in the rural counties of Wales. They can attend daytime meetings of county and district councils and national park committees, and used their muscle to oppose Cambrian Way. One wonders if those opposing the project had any idea of the satisfaction that many people derive from following a long continuous route on foot. For certain few, if any, had walked a long distance path - and that goes for most other opponents.

Other long distance paths were said to give farmers trouble, including Offa's Dyke, yet Offa's Dyke Association seldom hears of any problems. It hears much more from farmers wanting to be put on the bed and breakfast list. There are said to be 1250 farms providing accommodation and meals in Wales. Farm tourism means a lot to the economy of the uplands, and with farm subsidies now very much being questioned a second form of income, from path walkers, should be more than welcome .

I am sure that Cambrian Way walkers will be better behaved than the average tourist and holiday maker, if only because there will be little time to get up to mischief as there is an objective to be reached each day. In any case, those who have the strength of character to embark on an expedition such as the Cambrian Way are most unlikely to come from the strata of to-day's society that is involved in petty crime and vandalism. There are however "black sheep in every family" and some of the problems farmers suffer from are due to sheer ignorance or incompetence, so the following particular aspects of countryside behaviour are mentioned specifically.

Dogs. Whatever you do don't take a dog with you on the Cambrian Way. Dogs are the cause of more antagonism from farmers than any other cause. It is now an offence to walk with a dog in a field of sheep unless the dog is on a lead or "under close control" A farmer can shoot a dog worrying, or about to worry, livestock. Even the most placid of dogs can go berserk on seeing sheep and it is claimed that thousands of sheep are killed by dogs every year. Cattle dislike dogs and both bulls and cows with calves will chase them. Even if your dog is well behaved, you will be regarded with great suspicion by farmers. As far as I am concerned, no one who has had a dog with them will qualify for having walked the Cambrian Way.

Gates. A gate left open can cause the most awful problems. I heard of one farmer who brought several hundred sheep down to the valley the day before a contractors van was due to collect them. Someone left a gate open and not only did the van leave empty but the sheep got onto another farm and it took days to sort out the chaos. Remember farmers should not lock gates on a bridleway, so locking may not be the answer. Sometimes you find gates open. I do not entirely subscribe to the Country Code which tells you to shut all gates. You may be depriving animals of access to water. It is better to leave them as you find them, but if in doubt - shut. Leaders of parties should ask someone with them at the front to stay with the gate until the party is through, whether it has to be closed or not.

Rights of Way. Make certain that your map reading is impeccable so that you keep to the rights of way across farmland. Use both the Ordnance Survey maps and the maps in this guide and consult them frequently. Good map reading will be much more required than on, say, the Pennine Way. Avoid getting into the situation where you have to trespass to get back on course. Ensure that all members of a party have the necessary maps and can map read. Contour map reading is important, particularly at higher levels, and experience with this aspect may prove vital in cloud conditions.

Many farmers do not know where their rights of way are or may try to persuade you to go another way. If your right of passage is denied on what you believe to be a public right of way, use due discretion as to insisting on your rights. It is important to report such incidents to the county council and the Ramblers Association.

Nature Conservation

It speaks well for the defences built up by the nature conservation movement that the routing for the Cambrian Way was questioned in several places on conservation grounds. One had, however, to resist the almost automatic reaction of "You can't go that way - that's a nature reserve". One had to ask (a) what was it that was being conserved at that site, (b) what effect would Cambrian Way usage have on it, and (c) would that effect really matter? Generally the more knowledgeable the conservationist the more reasonable the answers received, and frequently it was clear that there was no real problem. One also concluded that the nature conservationists were often their own worst enemies in that they cannot keep secrets as to locations of rare species. Just as we were being told that a certain national nature reserve should be avoided, a radio broadcast was saying that this was the only place in the world that a certain tree grew. Walkers on the Cambrian Way are highly unlikely to be interested in identifying rare trees and digging them up. Nevertheless, I am not saying in this guide where that tree grows .

The red kite is not the only rare bird in Wales but was the only one mentioned as likely to be affected by the Cambrian Way, particularly in the Towy valley. This matter is covered more fully in the main text under "Rhandirmwyn". The effect in the nesting season of a few more walkers going up the Doethie valley will surely be very minimal.

Early in 1972 the Nature Conservancy offices at Bangor and Aberystwyth requested copies of the Cambrian Way Interim Report, which were sent with an offer to discuss any problems likely to arise on the routes concerned. In the autumn of that year, having heard nothing, I wrote to the Director of the Nature Conservancy asking for informal discussions. The reply, from the assistant director for Wales, was that discussions would be premature, so my attempts to become better informed were thwarted. No one can say I didn't try.

The Danger Aspects

It might be thought that one was proposing a walk over the highest peaks in the Alps to judge from some of the remarks passed about the dangers of the Cambrian Way. None of the summits traversed are technically difficult by the routes suggested for any normally healthy person, but of course any mountain can be a hazard in bad weather conditions, and the higher and steeper it is, the more the danger. Surely there is still scope for a spice of adventure in life. The critics point to the people who have to be rescued from the mountains because of ignorance of the basic requirements of equipment or because of foolhardiness in just not appreciating the hazards of venturing in the mountains. As with road safety, one can only go on plugging the need for care, rather than banning the pastime.

The attitude of many of the climbing fraternity was condescending to walkers to say the least. One statement made that particularly stuck in the gullet was that "paths should be laid out in areas of no interest to mountaineers". The attitude over use of the Rhinogs was near hysterical and akin to the sort of opposition Tom Stephenson had to his proposals to take the Pennine Way over Kinderscout. That wild moor was then forbidden territory. The northern Rhinogs provide a fantastic walk over rough and rocky ground, but in this case there is a public right of access to it, as it is Crown common. The national park authority would have the Rhinogs put in a glass case, labelled "Wilderness". Granted that such an area should not be developed for general tourist use but the one recreational use it is suitable for is a tough high level walk. If wilderness areas must be found, there are plenty of other parts of Wales that few want to go to which could qualify.

There was much pressure to work out a lower level alternative route, but really those who want such routes should follow other long distance paths and not try adulterating a natural high level route. The sort of compromises which were being proposed in the Brecon Beacons area just before abandonment were completely debasing the concept of a high level route. As a concession to mountain safety and as official long distance routes have to have specific routes designated, the Cambrian Way Committee put forward additional alternative routes for the Rhinogs, and for the Snowdon and Glyder areas, based on the precedent of official alternatives on the Pennine Way and Offa's Dyke. These have not been specified so precisely in this guide because there is much greater flexibility anyway with an unofficial route. Many alternatives are mentioned or are apparent from the Ordnance Survey maps

RIGHTS OF WAY AND ACCESS

It is important that walkers on the Cambrian Way should be conscious both of their right to proceed and of their obligations to those who live and work on the land they traverse. Whatever their rights, as detailed in the paragraphs below, they should always regard their travel over the land as a privilege given and accepted by persons mostly long since departed, and only occasionally due to recent negotiations.

A high proportion (161 miles = 59%) of the recommended routes are over public rights of way (also known as "highways"). There are varying degrees of public right of passage according to the status of the highway. If the way is a public footpath there is a right of way on foot. A bridleway has the additional right of riding or leading a horse or of riding a pedal cycle. "Roads used as public paths" may have vehicular rights of passage and "Byways open to all traffic" certainly have. These categories of highway are marked on the Ordnance Survey maps by different symbols, in red for the 1:50,000 scale and in green for the 1:25,000 Leisure and Pathfinder series . The O.S. gets its information from definitive maps of rights of way prepared by county councils and the existence of a path on the definitive map is conclusive evidence that it was a right of way at the relevant date of the definitive map. Legal orders changing rights of way have to be notified to the O.S. and should be taken account of at the next edition of the maps.

Public roads are mostly shown in various colours on the O.S. maps according to status but there are many public roads that are uncoloured. These "white" roads are mostly minor tarred roads or untarred stony roads or green lanes and are indistinguishable on the maps from private roads. With some the inference can be drawn that they are public if public paths are shown terminating on them. Cambrian Way uses several of these "white roads", checks on their status having been made at county highways offices.

The author has been particularly involved in the campaign over the last ten years to get all public roads marked as such on OS maps and at last there is a breakthrough. The No124 Landranger map entitled "Dolgellau", to be published in July 1995, is an experimental issue with open red diamond markings for "other routes with public access". The eastern approach to Mallwyd will be so marked. Tarred minor roads should all be marked in yellow.

Rights of way have become established by prolonged usage with the acquiescence of the owner of the land, and must be on a defined route. Although many public paths exist over open country it is common for the way to be less defined. When the survey of rights of way was being conducted from which the definitive maps were derived uncertainty as to the line of paths across open land often led to them being marked only to the edge of the open country. This was not thought to matter as the facility to roam at large was never disputed. This can however present problems if right of access is disputed. In English and Welsh law one cannot establish a right to roam at large by continued usage with acquiescence of the owner, as one can with defined rights of way. There are however some categories of open country where the public has a legal right of access and this has considerable relevance to the Cambrian Way.

Urban Commons

Under the Law of Property Act 1925 the public acquired a right of access for "air and exercise" to commons that at the time were administered by borough or urban district councils. At the south end of Cambrian Way this includes Mynydd Machen and a long line of commons from Twmbarlwm, near Newport, to the Blorenge near Abergavenny. At the north end Tal y Fan, Conwy Mountain and the exciting traverse path leading to the Sychnant Pass are on commons in former urban districts. 11½ miles of the Way are over non-definitive routes on urban commons.

Crown commons

Under the same act owners of common land were able to make a deed of declaration which gave the public the same rights of access over commons in former rural districts. In 1932 this procedure was adopted by the Crown Commissioners for its extensive commons in the rural districts of Wales (though not for England). Thus sections of the Cambrian Way, amounting to 11 miles, run over public access Crown commons, including the northern parts of the Carneddau, Plynlimon, the northern Rhinogs, Moelwyn Mawr, Domen Milwyn and Teifi Pools.

Difference between Rights of Way and Access

A right of way is a greater right over its width than a right of access. With a right of way the highway authority has a duty to maintain and to keep it free from obstruction. No such duty applies over the area of land to which the public may have access so that one cannot, for instance, expect bridges everywhere over streams or the clearing of gorse and bracken.

The Birmingham Clauses

The route passes over the fringe of the gathering grounds of the Elan Valley reservoirs which were built to supply Birmingham with water. The whole area is covered by the famous " Birmingham Clauses" which give "the public a privilege at all times to enjoy air, exercise and recreation". .

National Trust Land

Several sections of Cambrian Way traverse National Trust land which is open to the public. The longest stretch of non-definitive route on National Trust land is the high parts of the Carneddau from Ogwen to Drum. Other sections are on Sugar Loaf, Pen y Fan, and the Glyders - total 10 miles.

National Park Authority Land

It cannot be too often stressed that land in national parks is generally privately owned and that national park status does not give the public any additional right of access. In recent years however the Brecon Beacons National Park Authority has itself acquired certain large tracts of common land in order to ensure public access. This applies to the eastern section of Fforest Fawr (Great Forest) (see page 35) and the west side of the Black Mountain (see page 43). In 1989 it entered into a management agreement with Welsh Water for the western part of Forest Fawr (the east side of the Black Mountain.) This will safeguard public access on foot. These sections cover 12 miles (4½ %) of the main Cambrian Way route.

Forest Enterprise (formerly Forestry Commission)

Forest Enterprise allows general access on foot to its land subject to certain restrictions. Two sections of the Cambrian Way are on non definitive paths through such land. The OS is to resume marking of FE freehold land after a lapse of several years and the first map for this change is No124 (Dolgellau). There is a possibility that FE land will be sold and access restricted, but rights of way will remain. Please report any such access problems to the Ramblers Association and the author.

Cardiff

Cardiff City has no definitive map as yet but the route follows publically maintained paths and roads or is through public parks or a council owned former canal towpath open to the public.

Access under Tir Cymen Scheme

Tir Cymen, roughly translated means "a well crafted landscape", and is an experimental scheme in three parts of Wales under which farmers are paid in return for positive management of their land for the benefit of wildlife, landscape, archaeology and geology, and for providing better opportunities for quiet enjoyment of the countryside. If moorland or improved upland grassland is involved then public access must be allowed on foot for quiet enjoyment. It is similar to the Countryside Stewardship scheme in England but there is no direct payment for access. Four sections of Cambrian Way have such permissive access, under 10 year agreements, - from Bwlch Siglen to Cribin Fawr (page 60), part of the east approach to Cader Idris (62), and at Clip and Moel y Gyrafolen in the Rhinogs (66), a total of 5½ miles.

Countryside Council for Wales (as successors to the Nature Conservancy)

The CCW owns Cader Idris and the Rhinogs,Fawr and Fach, and allows general access to those very important mountains, with an emphasis on conservation.

Rural Commons

Commons in areas administered before 1974 by rural district councils do not provide a legal right of access for the public, unless there is a Law of Property Act deed. In practice the facility to roam is virtually never disputed. In 1986 the Common Land Forum reached a consensus view that there should be a legal right of access to all commons,subject to reasonable restrictions and rules of behaviour. This was later scuppered by grouse shooting interests in Scotland and the north of England, so blame them for lack of legal access to rural commons in Wales.

The longest stretch of rural common on the Cambrian Way is the Black Mountains section from Bal Mawr via the Tumpa, Waun Fach and Pen Allt Mawr to Table Mountain near Crickhowell. All this is very well known as a mountain walk. Another such section is Mynydd Llangynidr. On these commons there is "de facto" access and no one would dream of trying to find out who the owner was and asking permission to walk over them. Other large stretches of rural commons include Fforest Fawr and the Black Mountain, as referred to above.

Open Country Access Land

There remain five miles in four sections on high ground that do not fall into any of the above categories but which are open mountain country with de facto access, that is to say that so far as is known walkers are not denied access as long as they act in a reasonable manner - hopefully a situation that will long continue. Should problems arise over access at some time in the future there are provisions for securing legal access under the National Parks and Access to the Countryside Act 1949, either by agreement or compulsorily by order.

Other Non-Definitive Sections

New routes. In three instances waymarked paths are followed which have been negotiated by the National Park authorities. These may or may not be dedicated as rights of way.

Uncertain status routes. In two cases paths are followed which appear to be public but are not on the definitive maps or road plans. It may be that applications should be made for modification orders to add them to the definitive maps.

Courtesy Paths - this phrase, coined in Snowdonia, applies to certain negotiated routes such as the way from Pen-y-Pass to Glyder Fawr over open country in ownership of Mrs. Esme Kirby.

Unofficial Diversions. Frequently the route on the ground is different from the definitive route. A legal diversion should take place if it is a better route than the definitive line or the original route must be opened up if obstructed. A new right of way may have come about by twenty years use but the old way is still a right of way.

CAMBRIAN
WAY
SOUTH
Key to
1:50,000
Strip maps
and
O.S. Landranger
maps

29   30   Llanidloes

Devils
Bridge   135

28

27   Rhayader

25

26

24   147

Tregaron   23

22

146   Llanwrtyd   Builth

21   Hay

161

Llandovery   8

20   9

19   160   Brecon   10   7

16   15   14   11   6

17   18   17A   Ystrad-fellte   13   12   Abergavenny

Abercrave   5

Merthyr
Tydfil   Pontypool   4

171   3

Rhondda   Risca   Cwm-bran

170   Machen   2

Pontypridd   Caerphilly

Newport

1   Cardiff

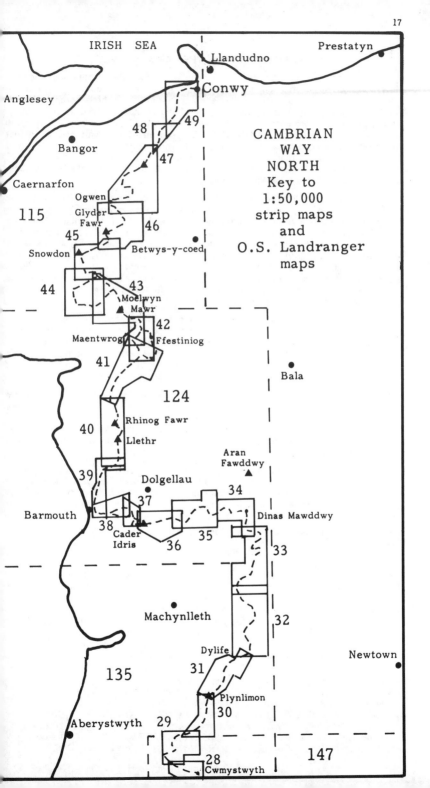

PLANNING TO WALK THE CAMBRIAN WAY

The main decision to be made is how one is to spend the nights in between the daily walking. The accommodation list in this guide gives addresses mostly of the bed and breakfast variety. Although youth hostels appear briefly in the geographical order of the list, a separate section gives details of the 20 hostels on or near the Way, which provide a more complete chain than the Pennine Way had even many years after its official opening. In parts of the Elenydd and Snowdonia hostels in fact provide the only accommodation available. The most serious gap is in the centre of the Rhinogs. Some other gaps are well covered by B.& B. but sections where accommodation is limited are the area to the north of Plynlimon and in the semi-industrialised valleys crossed near Newport.

The Cambrian Way is superb backpacking country provided the weather is kind, but Wales has an enormous rainfall in the mountains. However, the backpacker has greater freedom as to where to decide to stop and camp for the night. There are a few official camp sites en route and these are listed with the accommodation. It is most important that backpackers should get permission to camp on farmland and not take liberties that will upset relations with farmers who as a body fought vigorously against official designation of the Cambrian Way. It should be noted that there is no right to camp on common land and camping is specifically prohibited on National Trust land, water gathering grounds, and most other land to which the public has a right of access for air and exercise.

Those who are used to fell walking but not to carrying a big load over mountains should think twice before deciding to take camping equipment in case accommodation is not forthcoming. Cambrian Way has double the Pennine Way's ascent and can be wet under foot even in a dry summer. Wet feet and high loads are a sure recipe for blisters, not to mention problems of overbalancing on wet rocks, and possible ankle sprains miles from roads or habitation.

Don't make Cambrian Way your first long distance path, especially if you are backpacking and haven't carried camping gear before. Above all allow adequate time, at least three days more than for the Pennine Way, to allow for the extra ascent and remember there is a high dropout rate even on the Pennine Way. Cambrian Way is altogether a tougher proposition than other long distance paths in Britain and is through many remote areas with little or no public transport.

For further information on planning to walk the Cambrian Way turn to pages 78 to 96 at the end of the book.What follows on the succeeding pages is a general description and strip maps of the route, placed centrally in the book so that the pages can, if desired, be extracted for ease of reading while walking (see "Map carrying",page 81, also key to the strip maps on page 96)

TRANSPORT TO AND FROM THE CAMBRIAN WAY
RAIL
Cardiff, main lines from London, Midlands and the North.
Conwy, on main line - London, Crewe , Holyhead.
Heart of Wales line, - Shrewsbury *Llandovery*, Llanelli, Swansea (for Cardiff).
Cambrian Coast line, - Shrewsbury, Newtown, Machynlleth, Dovey Junc., *Barmouth*
    Llanbedr,Harlech,Portmadoc, (for Ffestiniog line), Pwllheli.
    Also Dovey Junction, Aberystwyth, (for *Devils Bridge* line).
Llandudno Junction, (1 mile from Conwy), to Blaenau Ffestiniog (2 miles from Way).
Cardiff,Newport,*Abergavenny*, Shrewsbury,Crewe,*Conwy.*
Ffestiniog line. Portmadoc,*Duallt*, Blaenau Ffestiniog. (01766 512340)
Note possible return route Conwy to Barmouth via Blaenau F. and Portmadoc.
COACH
National Express,- London, Shrewsbury, *Dyffryn Castell, Ponterwyd*, Aberystwyth
Daffodil line, - Shrewsbury, *Dinas Mawddwy*, Dolgellau, *Barmouth,* Tywyn
    Mon,Tue,Fri,Sat. Cambrian Coast Bus & Coachline, Tel 01654 711291
Trawscambria, - *Cardiff*, Swansea, Aberystwyth, Machynlleth, *Corris, Cross*
    Foxes, Dolgellau, *Trawfynydd, Maentwrog*, Caernarfon, Bangor, Holyhead.
    Crosville Wales, 01222 371331 or 01248 370295.Check re limited stops.
Machynlleth to *Dinas Mawddwy*, Crosville No 518, last bus about 15.45..

ROUTE DESCRIPTION AND STRIP MAPS

SOUTHERN SECTION
Cardiff to Llandovery
Via the Black Mountains & Brecon Beacons

Distance 107.5 miles(173km)   Ascent 21,163 feet (6455met)

The southern section of the Cambrian Way is the longer of the three sections into which the route naturally divides. Most of it is within the Brecon Beacons National Park which is entered just north of Pontypool, at 26 miles from the start. These non-national park miles are through the counties of South Glamorgan, Mid Glamorgan and Gwent, which were the only counties not to oppose the concept of the Cambrian Way.

Although Cardiff may sound like an unpromising start for a mountain walk it is possible by starting at the Castle to step straight into parkland and to follow a green belt between the built up area and the River Taff for over three miles before meeting a small industrial area. The M4 interchange crossing is horrific or fascinating according to taste but then the towers of Castell Coch beckon and one follows pleasant woodland and pastureland on the ridge between Cardiff and Caerphilly before crossing the ends of the famous mining valleys of Rhymney and Ebbw.The coalfield itself is by-passed to the south and east. The scenery in general is acceptable for a long distance path but in terms of the Cambrian Way is only a foretaste of better things to come.

Although the walk is rewarding it is not through a tourist area. It crosses industrial valleys where accommodation is relatively scarce.. Risca is about half way but most walkers would be advised to break themselves in by doing the Cardiff to Abergavenny stretch in 3 days.

Cardiff to Tongwynlais   5.4 miles   125 feet of ascent   Maps 1 & IA

As explained under "Maps" (page 80) it is assumed that the walker has the' 1:50,000 Ordnance Survey maps in addition to this guide. The description is not a stile by stile account and only serves to supplement the maps with useful information.

The first problem may be that the gates of Bute Park at the side of Cardiff Castle are not open until after early starters will have departed. However the west bank route through Sophia Gardens is almost equally attractive. Note the grotesque animal statues on the wall of the park between the Castle and Cardiff Bridge. Return to the east bank by suspension footbridge.

Easy wide paths lead along the riverbank, under Gabalfa Bridge (detour viar Llandaff Cathedral possible here to Llandaff Bridge. Turn away from the river after some sports grounds and make for a road going under a railway bridge. The next half mile is partly industrial but has some interest. First is the very tidy refuse disposal depot. Just beyond the Atlas Express depot a slight detour reveals a renovated old water wheel.. A picturesque industrial relic follows - the Glamorgan Canal, now a nature reserve. There is a choice of routes. Ahead to the right a stony drive is a public footpath leading onto the top of a steep bank of fine old woodland but the more interesting way is ahead left along the towpath of the old canal, a botanist' s paradise now in the care of the Cardiff City .The canal ends abruptly at an approach road to the Coryton interchange of the M4 . This "Spaghetti" junction provides the first real test of navigation as you negotiate two footbridges and two underpasses with the help of map 1A.. Be assured however that this is the only motorway to be encountered on the Cambrian Way.

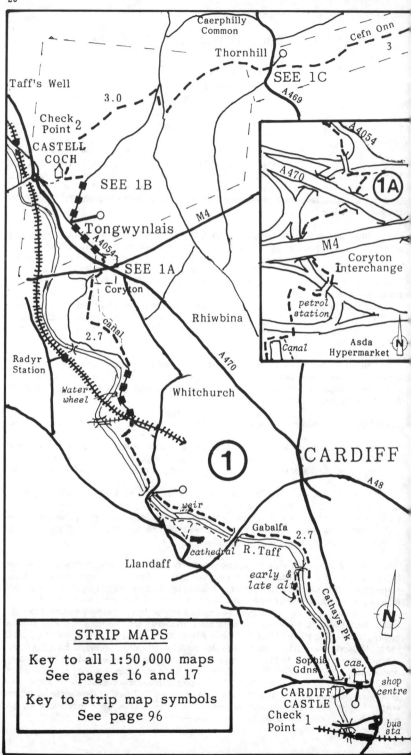

Caerphilly
Common

Cefn Onn

Thornhill

3

SEE 1C

Taff's Well

3.0

A469

Check
Point 2

CASTELL
COCH

A4054

A470

1A

SEE 1B

M4

Coryton
Interchange

Tongwynlais

A4054

SEE 1A

Coryton

petrol
station

canal

Rhiwbina

Asda
Hypermarket

Canal

N

2.7

A470

Radyr
Station

Water
wheel

Whitchurch

CARDIFF

A48

1

weir

Gabalfa

2.7

cathedral

R. Taff

Llandaff

early &
late alt

N

Cathays Pk

Sophia
Gdns

cas.

shop
centre

CARDIFF
CASTLE

Check
Point 1

bus
sta

STRIP MAPS

Key to all 1:50,000 maps
See pages 16 and 17

Key to strip map symbols
See page 96

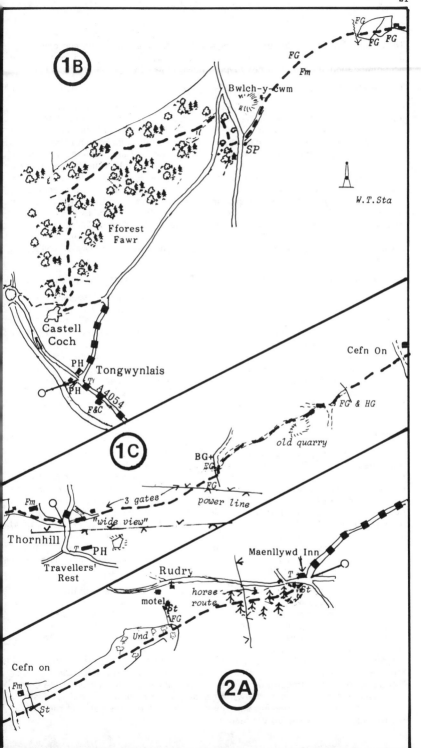

Tongwynlais has three pubs, two offering snacks at the bar, and a fish and chip shop. If a late start has been made from Cardiff, buses and trains can be taken for overnight accommodation in Cardiff, or Llwynypia Youth Hostel ,(see separate hostel list)

Tongwynlais to Machen   8.3 miles   875 feet of ascent   Maps 1, IB, IC, 2, 2A, 2B.

Walk up the road to the Castell Coch driveway, ignoring earlier signs off to the left. The castle *(Checkpoint No.2)* is a fairy tale style reconstruction of Victorian times, having been a complete ruin in 1870. The internal decor is lavish and worth a visit. A path up the bank behind the car park leads through Forestry Commission woodland. Keep to the main track, which unfortunately offers no views. Follow the inset map, which is shown in more detail near Thornhill where fields are crossed. Near an old quarry the view opens up to reveal Caerphilly with its large castle dimly discernible. The way continues to be well defined except in the wood beyond Cefn On. Beyond Rudry a dead end road leads into woods called Coed Cefn Pwll Du at grid reference 208871. Keep to the main forest road firstly north-east, then north, ignoring the first left forest road shown on the 1:50,000 map. Also ignore the bridleway marked on the map going northwards which does not exist on the ground. A view point with a seat shows the way ahead beyond Machen to Mynydd Machen, the next checkpoint.

Machen to Risca   3 miles   1022 feet of ascent   Maps 2, 2B & 2C

Mynydd Machen, the first definable summit on the route, is ascended by an evenly graded path up through forestry to reach open common. This is the first of several commons encountered on this section where the public have a right of access for "air and exercise" because the land was in an area administered before 1974 by an urban district council (see note page 14). From the stile onto the common there is no defined path up to the summit, where there is a trig point and radio station *(Checkpoint No.3)*. The fine panorama includes views across the Bristol Channel and up the mining valleys of Rhymney, Ebbw and Sirhowy. The way off is to follow the access road to the radio station, then by field and forest paths down to Risca. The reason for the apparently circuitous way down is that the direct route would be down very steep bracken covered hillside.

Risca to Pontypool   8.2 miles   1504 feet of ascent   Maps 2C, 3 & 3A

The crossing of the Ebbw Valley between Risca and Crosskeys is more populated than the Rhymney crossing at Machen , and has many of the typical features of the South Wales mining valleys. After a pleasant short section by the disused Monmouthshire and Brecon Canal, a plod up a dead end road leads to common land. At Pegwyn-y-bwlch one may be joined in the ascent of Twmbarlwm by walkers who have left their cars at a high point on the Cwmcarn Forest Drive. The ancient camp at Twmbarlwm is a worthy summit for a further checkpoint. *(No.4)* There is a problem of erosion here caused mainly by motor cyclists who have no right to ride on this common. Walkers, however, have a right of access as this is another common in a former urban district. One continues on this common nearly all the way to Pontypool .

Along the length of Mynydd Henllys the view to the right is onto the new town of Cwmbran, developed in the last forty years. It is the administrative centre of Gwent County. At the point where the forest on the left starts to vere from the ridge my preferred route keeps on the contour on a public footpath that is undefined on the ground, but peak baggers may prefer to keep on the track up to Mynydd Maen See the inset map for the short section off the common before the pleasant edge of common section round the woodlands surrounding the Blaen Blan reservoirs. Thirsty mountain walkers will not be able to resist a visit to a pub with the name of "Mountain Air Inn", although there is also a hospitable pub further on at the Lamb. The descent into Pontypool is down a narrow gated road to the north-east of the Larmb. Pontypool is a sprawling ugly town but do note the fine gates to the park at the mileage point marked on the map

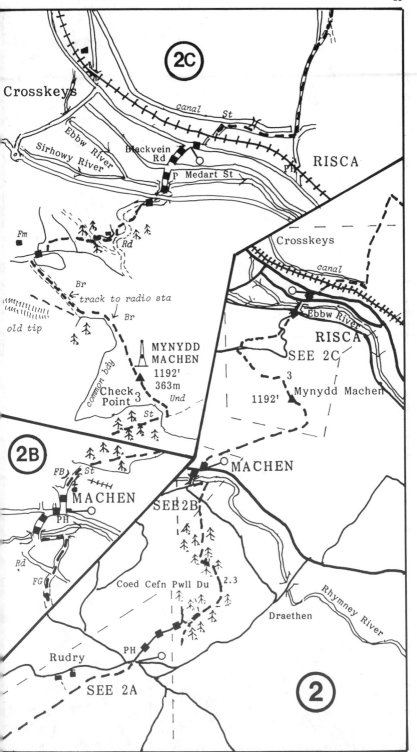

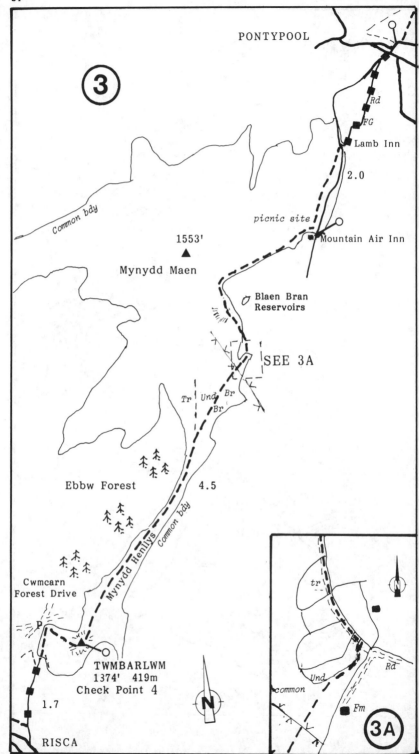

PONTYPOOL

③

Rd

FG

Lamb Inn

2.0

Common bdy

picnic site

Mountain Air Inn

1553'
▲

Mynydd Maen

Blaen Bran
Reservoirs

SEE 3A

Tr *Und* *Br*
Br

Ebbw Forest

4.5

Mynydd Henllys *Common bdy*

Cwmcarn
Forest Drive

P

TWMBARLWM
1374' 419m
Check Point 4

1.7

N

RISCA

tr

N

Und

Rd

common

Fm

③A

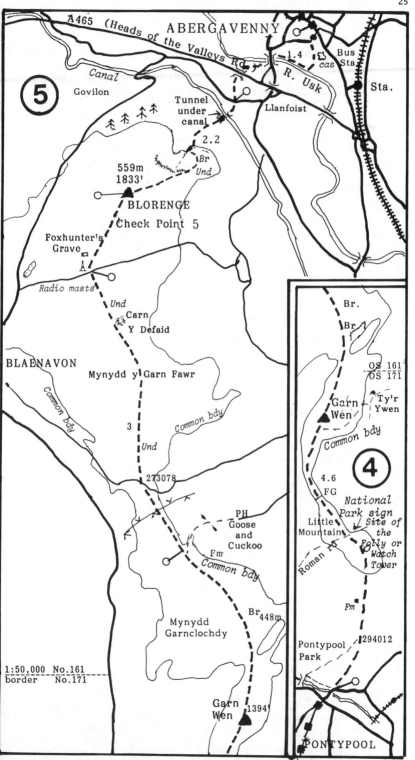

A465 (Heads of the Valleys Rd) ABERGAVENNY

Canal

Govilon

5

Tunnel under canal

1.4

cas

Bus Sta.

R. Usk

Sta.

Llanfoist

2.2

Br

Und

559m 1833'

BLORENGE

Check Point 5

Foxhunter's Grave

Radio masts

Und

Carn Y Defaid

BLAENAVON

Mynydd y Garn Fawr

Common bdy

3

Und

Common bdy

273078

PH Goose and Cuckoo

Common bdy

Fm

Mynydd Garnclochdy

Br 448m

1:50,000 No.161
border No.171

Garn Wen

1394'

Br.

Br.

OS 161
OS 171

Garn Wen

Ty'r Ywen

Common bdy

4

4.6

FG

National Park sign

Little Mountain

Site of the Folly or Watch Tower

Roman Rd

Fm

Pontypool Park

294012

PONTYPOOL

Pontypool to Abergavenny   11.3 miles   1691 ft. of ascent   Maps 4 & 5 .

The most pleasant amenity of Pontypool is the Park which can be entered by the palatial ornamental gates, enabling a detour to be made, rejoining the direct route at 294012. For the direct route mostly enclosed paths are followed to the site of the Pontypool Folly. From there, for most of the way to Abergavenny the route lies along open common land (all with a public right of access) with easy going for the first four miles, but after crossing a minor road at 273078 the going is over rough stony ground with no sign of the public right of way, then over heather and boulder land to the road by the radio masts.

Before taking the path from the east side of the car park, view the plaque which marks the grave of the famous horse Foxhunter. From the trig. point summit head north-east for half a mile to the spectacular viewpoint over Abergavenny. There is a direct but very steep and eroded path down the centre of a north-east face of Blorenge but a better way is just north of east, down through bracken covered hillside and curving round to an isolated tree (not visible until lower down) whence follow a narrow path to the aforementioned direct way down. Descent to the River Usk crossing is on the line of an old tramway incline which goes through a tunnel where it passes under the Monmouthshire and Brecon Canal.

Abergavenny (ECD Thur.) is an important gateway from England into South Wales, and abounds in B.&B. and eating places. The B.&B. is mostly in two areas of the town, namely on the A40 going south-east, near the bus and railway stations and on A40 going west. The information bureau is at the bus station .

The Black Mountains

Since the early planning stages of the Cambrian Way there have been arguments whether the Black Mountains should be included. The writer has always argued for inclusion because of the sheer excellence of the ridge walking they provide.

The Countryside Commission at first included them in the draft proposals but bowed to pressure from the National Park authority. When the project officer was appointed for the southern third of the Way, he was not asked to investigate any route over the Black Mountains. The Park's reasons for exclusion of the Black Mountains were based on their conservation importance and sensitivity, and because of the de facto access availability to walkers. This seems to be a "can't win" situation since if there had been no access this would also, no doubt, have been given as a reason for non-inclusion.

The Black Mountains have suffered greatly from erosion caused by horse riding, and only to a lesser extent by the feet of walkers. The area around the summit of Waun Fach may never recover its grass cover. The eroded approach to the summit of Sugar Loaf can be by-passed without causing such wear that would widen the gashes. One must accept a bare earth path for much of the way but this is not the sort of erosion problem that besets the Pennine Way with its peat bogs.

A frequent criticism of inclusion of the Black Mountains is that two days after leaving Abergavenny one is only four miles away at Crickhowell. This is a valid point and aggravating to the beeliners who only want to get from one end of Wales to the other, to say they have "done it". For our connoisseur of mountain walking the quality of the walking and the scenery is what counts. It would be a crime to omit the Black Mountains .

Many prospective Cambrian Way walkers will have followed the Offa's Dyke Path and will recall having trudged along the 12 miles of the Hatterall Ridge.It's hard

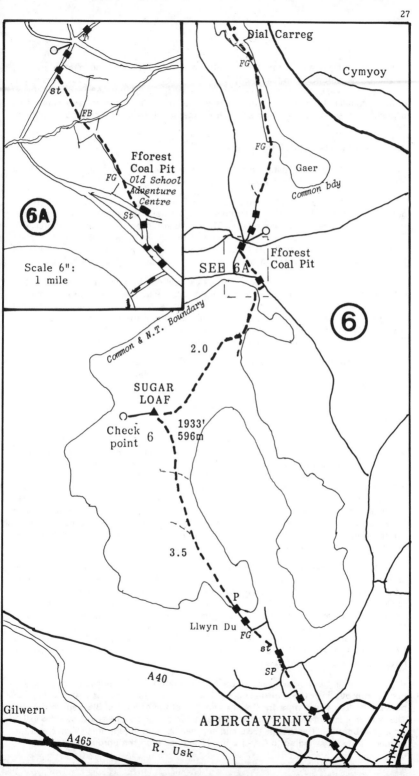

luck on Offa's Dyke walkers that their route follows the longest and least interesting of the Black Mountain ridges. Cambrian Way follows most of the good ridges, but never for too long in one direction or without some up and down. Whereas the slopes of the Hatteral Ridge curve to prevent views into the valleys immediately below, the opposite is true of the Bal Mawr and Pen Alltmawr ridges from which both near and distant views are superb.

Alternative Routes to Black Mountains

If despite the foregoing paragraphs the reader decides to by-pass the Black Mountains, there are several possibilities, as follows:

1. From Blorenge to Mynydd Llangattock, crossing the B4246 at Pen-ffordd-goch Pond (255108) and proceeding across open common land to Llam-march and to Cwm Clydach national nature reserve. The dramatic gorge is crossed by the Devil's Bridge thence by subway under the Heads of the Valleys road (A465) to the Drum and Monkey Inn at Blackrock. The escarpment of the east and north sides of Mynydd Llangattock can be followed to rejoin the main route at Daren Cilau (200159).

2. The towpath of the Brecon and Usk Canal can be followed from the tunnel referred to in the text at 285130 to Llangattock, near Crickhowell. Said to be the most attractive canal in Britain, it has been much restored for pleasure boating and its towpath is well maintained by the national park authority. On this six mile stretch the canal twists and turns as it follows the contours round the hillside some 150 to 200 feet above the river Usk, with consequent good views across the valley.

3. From the summit of Sugar Loaf to Crickhowell either via Mynydd Pen-y-fal and Llangenny or via Cwm Gwenffrwd, Cwrt-ygollen and riverside walk to Crickhowell Bridge.

Abergavenny to Capel-y-ffin via Sugar Loaf and Bal Mawr
13 miles   3443 feet of ascent   Maps 6 to 8

The recommended way out of Abergavenny from the Town Hall Clock Tower is along the main street, thence via Pound Road and Avenue Road to Llwyn Du. One is spoilt for choice as to ways up Sugar Loaf from Abergavenny. There are pleasant routes up the east side of the Rholben ridge and up the ridge itself but the author's preferred route is up St. Mary's Vale on the west side of that ridge. The path ascends gradually from a small car park onto the open bracken covered common. Sugar Loaf has public right of access both because it is a common in a former urban district and because it is National Trust land open to the public. Keep on ascending path until the broad ridge is gained then follow paths to the summit, avoiding the badly eroded south-west flank (which leads in from the highest car park).

Leave Sugar Loaf by the north-east ridge again taking care not to cause further erosion near the top. A short lane connects the common to a minor road at Fforest Coal Pit (charcoal, not the black variety) whence paths and minor roads are followed to Dialgarreg where the splendour of the Black Mountain ridges begins to be apparent as one looks down on the right to the Vale of Ewyas and to the left the forested Grwyne Fawr. Across the former valley is the crooked church at Cwmyoy, where the chancel tilts one way and the tower another. In the latter valley, and worth a detour from the cross roads at Fforest if time permits, is the isolated church of Partrishow, noted for its rood loft with beautiful carved oak screen, (279224).

Continuing over Garn Wen to Bal Mawr, the ridge becomes narrower and the views improve into the contrasting valleys on either side. About half a mile after passing the forest turn right for Capel-y-ffin at a stone called the Blacksmith's Anvil. The way is at first none too apparent but then becomes a steep track down the valley side. Pass between The Grange (B&B and inquiries about camping further on) and the former monastery, and so to Capel-y-ffin (The chapel on the border). *Check Pt. 7*

Hay Bluff

Lord Hereford's Knob
TWMPA
2263' 690m
Check
Point 8

Gospel Pass

Und

Hostel variant

2.5

2.9

Common bdy

1.1

(8)

SEE 8A

Check
Point 7
CAPEL-Y-FFIN
1040'
327m

und

cairn

3.9

(8A)

Scale
6":1 mile
(1:10560)

N

The
Grange

The Monastery

N

Hatterrall Ridge

Offa's Dyke Path

Vale of Ewyas

Afon Honddu

Common boundary

Chwarel
y Fan
2228'

Bal
Mawr
*pile of
stones*

Bal
Bach

N

common bdy

Garn
Wen
*tall
cairn*

3.7

(7)

Dial
Garreg

Grwyne Fawr

Bal Mawr
1991'

Llanthony

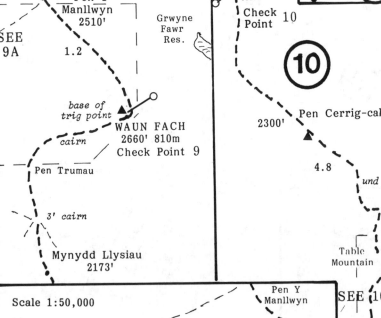

30

TWMPA
2263' 690m

und

Mynydd Llysiau

Table Mountain

4.3

2.8

Blaen Grwyne-fawr

und

9

two slabs

Pent-wynglas

FG
St
FG
St
FG
St
St
St
Fm

Waymarked path

10A

Pen Y Manllwyn
2510'

SEE 9A

1.2

Grwyne Fawr Res.

2360' Pen Allt-mawr Check Point 10

10

base of trig point

WAUN FACH
2660' 810m
Check Point 9

cairn

Pen Trumau

2300' Pen Cerrig-calch

4.8

und

3' cairn

Mynydd Llysiau
2173'

Table Mountain

Scale 1:50,000

Pen Y Manllwyn

SEE 10A

2.7   Y Grib

9A

Waun Fach

1060'   Castell Dinas

Pengenffordd
Castle Inn

900'   A 479

CRICKHOWELL

P

This idyllic spot at the junction of steep sided valleys was initially an idea for the starting place for the Cambrian Way. It was soon apparent that this was no equivalent of Edale on the Pennine Way and needed easier lines of communication.

For those anxious to see the impressive ruins of Llanthony Abbey and prepared to forgo the pleasures of the Bal Mawr ridge a descent can be made from Bal-bach (273267) . After visiting the abbey and possibly calling or staying at the Half Moon Inn, follow the very minor roads and tracks on the NE side of the river Honddu via Broadley and the Vision Farm to Capel-y-ffin. The main road up the valley is narrow with high hedges and not recommended for walking.

Capel-y-ffin to Crickhowell via Twmpa, Waun Fach and Pen Allt Mawr Ridge
16 miles   2652 feet of ascent   Maps 8 to 10

A section of very narrow road and a field path leads back to the open common whence the main route to Twmpa and the hostel variant divide. If going to the hostel, this way is preferable to the suicidal road route to the gate below the hostel. The Youth Hostel is a friendly old farmhouse with resident warden and is rather special in that it was provided by the King George VI Memorial Fund, which provided one hostel each in England, Scotland and Wales The route from the hostel to Twmpa is via a steep climb at the back of the hostel and a superb viewpoint looking down the Vale of Ewyas.

Twmpa, also known as Lord Hereford's Knob, is check point number 8 . This splendid viewpoint on the N W. escarpment of the Black Mountains looks out across the wide valley of the Wye to the hillls of central Wales . Two miles away to the NE is Hay Bluff, as near as Cambrian Way gets to the Offa's Dyke Path. In between is the Gospel Pass over which the icecap of the Great Ice Age overflowed to make the Vale of Ewyas the only glaciated valley of the Black Mountains.

From Twmpa to Waun Fach a path is well worn along the open common except after crossing the old track coming up from Grwyne Fawr where there are several rival paths. A compass will certainly by needed in mist. From just short of Pen y Minllwyn (small cairn) a diversion can be made down Y Grib to Pengenffordd and the Castle Inn. The summit of Waun Fawr is on a flat plateau and not exactly impressive as the highest point in the Black Mountains. It is check point number 9 but our Mountain Connoisseur is excused having to walk to the actual base of the former trig. point provided a wide circuit is taken round it, well beyond the summit area, which is devoid of vegetation due to too many feet ,both human and equine.

The eroded parts of the slope going westwards from Waun Fach can be by-passed without causing more erosion. Superb ridge walking follows over Mynydd Llysiau, Pen Allt-mawr and Pen Cerrig-calch before descent to the curious Table Mountain, an iron age hill fort, which is aptly named. The open common is left just below Table Mountain at 225203 and waymarked field paths followed (see map 10A) to a road leading into Crickhowell.

Crickhowell is a small town with many scheduled buildings. One of these was the Youth Hostel but regrettably serious structural defects were discovered which were beyond the resources of the YHA to remedy, causing its closure in 1982. There is, however, ample B &B, a good camp site, and many pubs providing meals.

Crickhowell to Storey Arms via Mynydd Llanynidr and Pen y Fan
20 miles & 4896 feet of ascent via Torpantau Pass (+ 1.7 miles to Llwyn y celyn YH) or 13.9 miles(1808ft) and 10.7miles (3865ft), using the Talybont variant.

Crickhowell Bridge, over the Usk, is a gem of an old stone bridge. From it a path leads over fields to Llangattock church and thence up to the Brecon and Usk Canal, the towpath of which is followed for half a mile, as far as the second bridge. An old tramway route, at first on the flat, then up a very steep incline, leads to the area of the former Llangattock quarries. The next two miles provide some of the most spectacular scenery on the whole Cambrian Way. The area is a nature reserve. An old

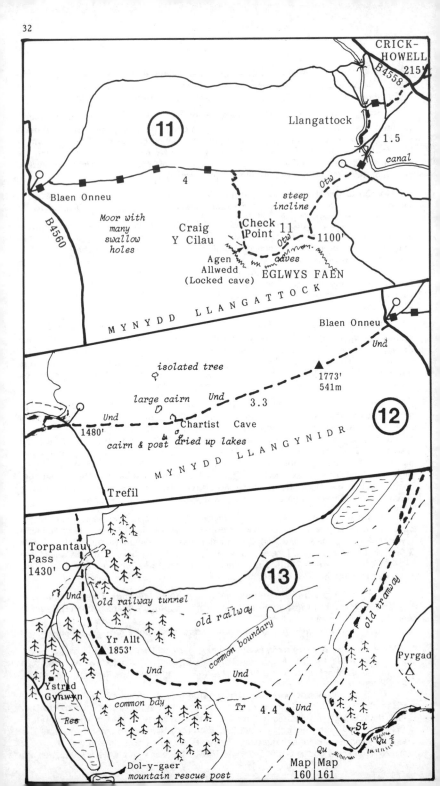

CRICK-
HOWELL
B4558
215'

11

Llangattock

1.5

canal

Blaen Onneu

4

steep
incline

B4560

Moor with
many
swallow
holes

Craig
Y Cilau

Check
Point

11

1100'

Otw

Otw

Agen
Allwedd
(Locked cave)

caves

EGLWYS FAEN

M Y N Y D D   L L A N G A T T O C K

Blaen Onneu

Und

isolated tree

1773'
541m

large cairn

Und

3.3

12

Und

1480'

Chartist   Cave

cairn & post dried up lakes

M Y N Y D D   L L A N G Y N I D R

Trefil

Torpantau
Pass
1430'

P

13

Und

old railway tunnel

old railway

old tramway

Yr Allt
1853'

common boundary

Pyrgad

Und

Und

Ystrad
Gynwyn

Und

common bdy

Tr   4.4   Und

Res

St

Qu

Dol-y-gaer
mountain rescue post

Map
160

Map
161

tramway route on a ledge below Darren Cilau leads to a spot where a short scramble gives access into a large open cave, Eglwys Faen, which can be explored with a torch and considerable care. *(Check point no. 11.)* A different proposition is Agen Allwedd cave which is many miles long and only accessible to those with a key. Near to Agen Allwedd entrance a path gradually descends off the main ledge to the base of the cliff and to an area of springs and swamp before reaching the Llangattock - Blaen Onneu road. One can walk along the grassy common land rather than the road itself.

From the road junction at Blaen Onneu across Mynydd Llangynidr is a very wild and open moor, over which careful navigation is essential, even with good visibility. This is cave country with many swallow holes and sheep tracks, but few defined paths. The rights of way do not help but de facto access is traditional here.The first objective is the trig. point at 148159 but more difficult to find is the Chartist Cave, where clandestine presses printed forbidden political papers a century and a half ago. Cairns and an isolated tree provide clues but in mist only good compass and contour navigation will enable the socialist pilgrim to find the wide open cave, facing south, and appreciate this inhospitable shelter. If the cave can be easily missed at least one should strike the road to Hendre and Ystrad quarries. Keep away from the quarries and follow the line of an old tramroad between the quarries and the top of the drop into the very steep sided valley of Dyffryn Crawnon. At a stile the main route and the Talybont Variant divide, the variant continuing on the tramroad while the main route turns left before the stile and hugs the fence round the edge of the quarry area until the open common is gained, whence strike across open moor to the ridge of Yr Allt and so down to Torpantau Pass.

From Torpantau to Pen y Fan, the highest point in the Brecon Beacons, the obvious and popular route is via Craig y Fan-ddu, Craig Cwareli and Cribin. The first of several eroded sections on this route is the ascent of Craig y Fan-ddu. This seems to have been aggravated by putting a car park in the forest near Torpantau Pass, but our Cambrian Way walker will add little to the erosion if discretion is exercised in using either the worn track or avoiding it. At a stream (050192) a line is struck across the wild moorland top for half a mile to meet the crag-top path at Craig Cwareli.

The Talybont Variant has been added to this edition to facilitate a break up of the Crickhowell to Storey Arms section. The tramroad can be followed all the way to Talybont-on-Usk, a hospitable village on the Brecon & Usk canal, or a steeper way followed down through forest to Talybont Reservoir and Aber Village where there is B&B and a small campsite. To save a major reshuffle of pages, map 13A for the variant is on page 58.

From Craig Cwareli,where the routes rejoin, to Pen y Fan and on to Storey Arms, the paths are all very worn, including short cuts of Fan Big and Cribin. The purists will visit all the summits but only Pen y Fan has been made a check point so as not to discourage the less eroded alternative described below. It is the south-east ridge of Pen y Fan which provides the National Park with its most intractable erosion problem, and which seems only likely to be solved by a concession to artificiality in some form of steps if the mountain is not to be gradually worn away. However Pen y Fan will not disappear for a few million years yet, so if you want to follow the most spectacular cragtop route in the Brecon Beacons you must accept the erosion eyesores and your contribution to gradual lowering of the mountains.

There is an alternative between Torpantau and Pen y Fan along the long and less interesting cragtop ridge accessible from the base of the lower Neuadd reservoir and passing along Craig Fan Ddu (no connection with crag three paragraphs ago), and Bwlch Duwynt . This route, often used as a return on a horseshoe ascent of Pen y Fan from Torpantau, was put forward in Mr. Tetlow's report as a suggested route for Cambrian Way. The owners, National Trust and Forestry Commission, were said to be agreeable. There was a naive assumption that the summit of Pen y Fan would be by-passed, but at least if it is visited the south-east ridge up it is avoided.

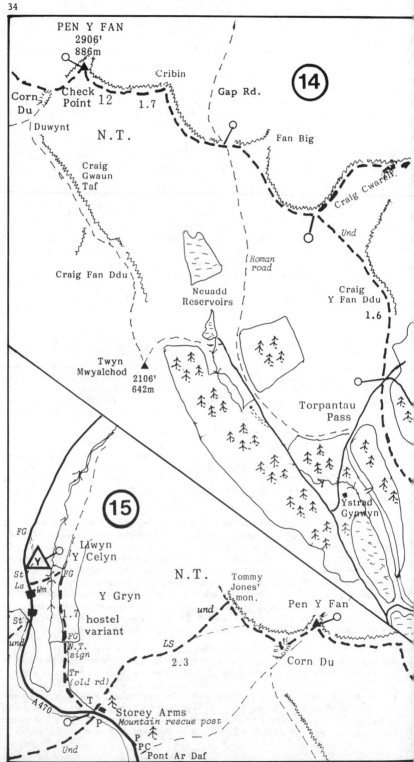

PEN Y FAN
2906'
886m

Cribin

Gap Rd.

⑭

Corn
Du

Duwynt

Check
Point 12   1.7

Fan Big

N.T.

Craig
Gwaun
Taf

Craig Cwarelp.

Und

Craig Fan Ddu

Roman
road

Neuadd
Reservoirs

Craig
Y Fan Ddu
1.6

Twyn
Mwyalchod
2106'
642m

Torpantau
Pass

Ystrad
Gynwyn

⑮

FG

Llwyn
Y Celyn

St
Ls   Wm

FG

Y Gryn

N.T.

Tommy
Jones'
mon.

Pen Y Fan

St

und

1.7
hostel
variant

FG

und

LS

N.T.
sign

Tr
(old rd)

LS
2.3

Corn Du

A470

T

Storey Arms
Mountain rescue post

P

P
PC
Pont Ar Daf

Und

There is no need to follow the grossly overused and eroded path from Bwlch Duwynt to the A470 at Pont ar Daf. More rewarding is to come off the west side of the summit plateau of Corn Du and follow the north-west ridge down to an obelisk. This is a memorial to Tommy Jones who, aged five, got lost while staying at a farm in the valley, and whose body was found at that spot nearly a month later. The more popular route leaves the ridge before the memorial, but both routes cross the valley to a ladder stile, and so by path down to Storey Arms. The former pub which gives its name to this important road pass has long since gone, so that any sustenance here is more likely to be from an ice cream van. Part of the Outdoor Education Centre at the pass used to be a Youth Hostel but now the hostel in this area is a converted farmhouse 1¾ miles towards Brecon in less bleak surroundings. A quieter route to it than the busy trunk road is along the old road on the east side of the valley and then by a permissive route across National Trust land from 977222 to 972221.

Storey Arms to Llandovery via Fforest Fawr and the Black Mountain
22.6 miles   4955 ft of Ascent   Maps 16 to 20

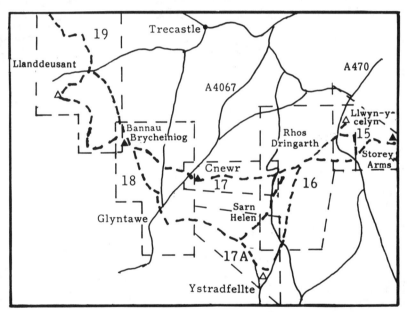

Map showing the relationship of the alternative routes between the Brecon Beacons and the Black Mountain (Carmarthen Vans), and the strip maps involved

Fforest Fawr (Great Forest) is not forest in the modern sense but is large open moorland. It is in two main sections. The eastern part is between the Brecon to Merthyr road (A470) and the minor road from Heol Senni to Ystradfellte. Another large section is on the east side of the main ridge of the Black Mountain with Bannau Brycheiniog part way along its open boundary with the Black Mountain common. These enormous commons are used for grazing by many farmers from the surrounding area. In February 1984, the National Park authority purchased the eastern part and several other sections from the Eagle Star Insurance Company for £30,000, with the help of grants from the National Heritage Memorial Fund and the Countryside Commission. The purpose of this very welcome purchase was to protect the commons, to conserve the open hill landscape and also the access on foot which the public has enjoyed in practice, if not as of right, for many years.

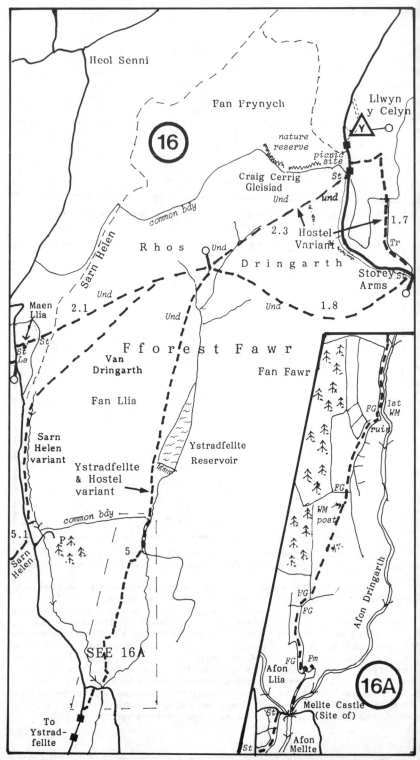

Heol Senni

Fan Frynych

16

nature reserve

picnic site

Llwyn y Celyn

Y

Craig Cerrig Gleisiad

St

Und

Und

Rhos

Und

1.7

Tr

2.3 Hostel Variant

D r i n g a r t h

Storey's Arms

St

Sarn Helen

common bdy

Maen Llia

2.1

Und

Und

Und

1.8

St

St Ls

F f o r e s t   F a w r

Van Dringarth

Fan Faw

Fan Llia

Sarn Helen variant

Ystradfellte Reservoir

Ystradfellte & Hostel variant

1st WM

FG

ruin

FG

WM post

common bdy

5.1

P

5

FG

Sarn Helen

FG

Afon Dringarth

SEE 16A

FG

Fm

Afon Llia

Mellte Castle (Site of)

St

16A

To Ystradfellte

St

Afon Mellte

Check
Point 13A
FAN
GIHIRYCH
2379'
725m

17

tower St
und

new forestry
Bwlch
Y Duwynt
cairn

4.2
und FG
und

CNEWR ROUTE
(NOT APRIL 15TH TO MAY 10TH)

und
cairn und

Fan Nedd

To Heol Senni

Maen
Llia
Llech
Llia
LS

1 mile gap

4.0

NCC
notice
St
wall

*old wall
enclosures* →

int

ruin
Und
Tr

new forestry
Sarn Helen
Maen
Madoc
(standing
stone)

BLAEN NEDD ISAF
Check Point 13 B

1.9

SEE 17B
YSTRADFELLTE

P
Afon
Llia

17A

SARN HELEN AND
YSTRADFELLTE VARIANTS

Scale 1:50,000

Blaen Nedd
Isaf
FG St
FG
FB
St
St
FG
FG ind

*limestone
pavement*

FG *tr*
1.9

Fm

P

Pwll Y Rhyd
caves

canyon

FG

FG

SnRd

FG

YSTRADFELLTE
inn
P PO
PC

17B

1:25,000

River Neath
Afon Nedd

*river
bed
usually
dry*

cave

Porth Yr Ogof

The Cnewr Estate. In the north centre of Fforest Fawr, and including the natural east/west walking route, is the privately owned enclosed moorland of the Cnewr Estate. Lambing on sheep farms generally takes place in late winter, near to farmhouses in the valleys, but when the Cnewr land was first enclosed many years ago the estate had no land in the valleys. Lambing was therefore carried out in springtime on the open mountain. Due to possible disturbance by walkers and risk of sheep worrying by dogs the estate has generally not encouraged access, particularly at lambing time. When the estate applied for permission to plant parts of the moor with conifers in 1980 the National Park made a deal with the estate to reduce its demands and to allow access across the estate by two routes, including an east/west route via Fan Nedd, Fan Gihirych and Cefn Cul. Access is however not allowed between April 15th and May 10th , the lambing season, and is not allowed at night. Organised parties have to notify the National Park Authority in advance. Dogs must be kept on leads and no fires are permitted. Rough camping for backpackers is allowed near the ruined building of Llech Llia. During the lambing season a detour can be made via the Roman road Sarn Helen and Glyntawe, or the journey broken at Ystradfellte, as described below.

Storey Arms or Llwyn-y-celyn to Rhos Dringarth. Map 16.

Cnewr ,Sarn Helen and Ystradfellte routes leave Storey Arms and head west for Fan Fawr which can be ascended or by-passed on the northern side. If coming from Llwyn-y-celyn Youth Hostel, leave the hostel grounds at the S.W. corner and follow roadside verge of A470 for 400 yards then over stile and climb obliquely south-west onto the wide featureless expanse of Rhos Dringarth.

Rhos Dringarth to Bannau Brycheiniog via Fan Gihirych (Cnewr Estate)

Maps 16, 17 and 18. Once on the broad expanse of the rhos (moorland) strike generally south westwards. From the broad ridge between Cefn Perfedd and Fan Dringarth head towards the large standing stone, Maen Llia. A rough track, which is an old Roman road called Sarn Helen, is crossed shortly before reaching a wall. This is the edge of the Cnewr Estate. A new stile invites one to cross the small enclosed section of moor to the standing stone and thence over a stile onto the Heol Senni to Ystradfellte road. A few yards south a ladder stile indicates the start of the permissive route across the Cnewr moors. *(Not between April 15th and May 10th)*. Head for the summit of Fan Nedd, then north west to Bwlch y Duwynt and Fan Gihirych.

From the summit of Fan Gihirych there is a very steep drop to Bwlch Bryn-rhudd, the road pass on A4067, so that it is necessary in the interests of safety and prevention of erosion to follow the edge southwards until the slope becomes easier and then to strike northwest to the bwlch. (Do not follow the suicidal descent route shown on Leisure map 12) The route continues on Cnewr land over Cefn Cul passing near a curious tower. Old walls and fence posts are useful for navigation across the bleak moor, and it is important to arrive at the ladder stile near Maen Mawr and stone circle because there is no other crossing of the high wall and barbed wire fence which marks the western boundary of the Cnewr Estate. (853203)

Once again one is on open land section of Fforest Fawr where there is de facto access. Crossing the Tawe can be tricky - if necessary cross higher up. Head for the south end of Llyn y Fan Fawr (not visible until almost there) then on the obvious path up the crags to Bwlch y Giedd and thence to the summit of Bannau Brycheiniog, 2630 feet, 802m, *(Check point 14)*, the highest point in the Carmarthen Vans. If in luck you will look back to the other peaks that have been ascended en route.

Alternative routes avoiding the Cnewr Estate. Maps 16, 17A & 18.

1. Via Ystradfellte. If an extra day can be spared then this variation is worth while on its own account because of the opportunity to spend at least a half day exploring the beautiful valleys around Ystradfellte with their famous waterfalls and caves. This assumes that a night is spent at Ystradfellte.

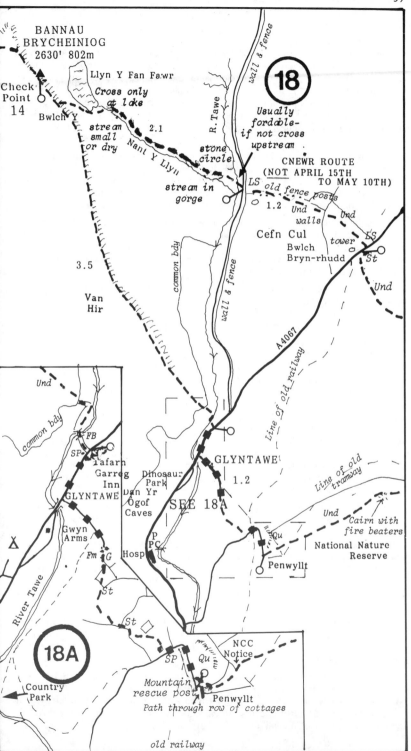

BANNAU
BRYCHEINIOG
2630' 802m

Llyn Y Fan Fawr
*Cross only
at lake*

Check
Point
14

Bwlch Y

*stream
small
or dry*

Nant Y Llyn

2.1

R. Tawe

wall & fence

18

*Usually
fordable -
if not cross
upstream.*

*stone
circle*

CNEWR ROUTE
(NOT APRIL 15TH
TO MAY 10TH)

*stream in
gorge*

LS *old fence posts*

1.2 Und
walls Und

Cefn Cul

Bwlch
Bryn-rhudd tower LS
St

Und

common bdy

3.5

Van
Hir

wall & fence

A4067

Line of old railway

Und

FB

SP

Tafarn
Garreg
Inn

GLYNTAWE

Dan Yr
Ogof
Caves

Dinosaur
Park

GLYNTAWE

1.2

Line of old tramway

Gwyn
Arms

Fm G

St

Hosp

P
PC

SEE 18A

Und

Qu

Cairn with
fire beaters

National Nature
Reserve

Penwyllt

St

18A

St

SP Qu

NCC
Notice

Country
Park

River Tawe

common bdy

Und

*Mountain
rescue post*
Path through row of cottages Penwyllt

old railway

From Rhos Dringarth take a wide sweep round the moor, crossing several small tributaries of the Dringarth and then head south to pass along the west side of the Ystradfellte reservoir. Once past the dam drop down to the river and where a fence comes down from the west, turn alongside the river at 943168 and scramble between the river and the fence for about 400 yards to a gate where a waymarked public bridleway starts, near Blaen-tringarth at 942164. This is the only right of way off this part of the common and must be followed precisely. The waymarking is yellow Countryside Commission shape arrows and ends at the road near the site of Castell Coch.

Ystradfellte. The solubility of the carboniferous limestone hereabouts has caused the rivers Mellte, Hepste and Nedd (Neath) to go underground, sometimes completely and in other parts for all except flood time. Alternate layers of hard and soft rocks have also caused waterfalls. Add to that the steep sided valleys clothed in natural woodlands and you have a wonderland of great interest and beauty.

If arriving from the Storey Arms area in the middle of the day one can, before spending the night, have a rewarding half day proceeding down the Mellte valley via Porth yr Ogof (large open cave) and the three Clun Gwyn falls to Sgwd yr Eira on the Hepste river. This latter is a waterfall with a public footpath that passes between the waterfall and the cliff it shoots over.

If two nights can be spent at Ystradfellte, a day is recommended exploring also the valleys of the Nedd, Sychryd and Pyrddin, especially if the rivers are low enough for walking along riverbeds. The cave systems should be treated with great respect, and only entered by experienced cavers with the appropriate equipment.

Ystradfellte to Glyntawe.   Maps 17A,17B,18 & 18A
Routes from the youth hostel and from the area of the pub car park and church converge in a field at 920139 and then go west, past an interesting limestone pavement on the way to Blaen Nedd Isaf Farm. Go through a gate at the south end of the row of buildings. Sarn Helen, an old Roman road is crossed at 908144. Here starts a public footpath that traverses a wild open moor without touching any other highway for four miles . The 1: 50, 000 map shows little to guide one but the walls and small enclosures on the sketch map should more than suffice for navigation. The western half of the path is through a national nature reserve noted for its cave systems. The moorland path ends at a line of cottages forming a caving centre for the South Wales Caving Club.(Mountain Rescue Post) A disused railway is crossed at the Penwyllt quarries and a signpost followed on what appears to be an unofficial diversion at the start of a path down to Glyntawe.

Glyntawe, apart from being a scattered community in a very attractive valley, is noteworthy for the Dan yr Ogof Caves, claimed to be the largest showcave complex in Europe, and for Craig y nos Castle, an enormous Gothic style chateau where, at the turn of the last century Madame Adelina Patti, the famous opera singer provided lavish entertainment and was a frequent host to royalty. The castle is now a geriatric hospital but most of the fine grounds form a country park open to the public. An alternative path from Penwyllt via Rhongyr-uchaf gives access to the park at 843157. If time permits the caves should be visited and also the life size dinosaur park.

Glyntawe to Bannau Brycheiniog. Opposite the Tafarn-y-Garreg Inn a path leads to a footbridge and thence to the open common at 848173. The rough stone strewn hillside is climbed and the escarpment followed for three miles to its highest point at Bannau Brycheiniog.

2. Alternative to the Cnewr Estate via Sarn Helen. Maps 16,17A,17B,18, 18A. If seeking to avoid the Cnewr Estate but not wishing to go to Ystradfellte, take a more south-westerly line from Rhos Dringarth so as to hit the road where it is joined by Sarn Helen at 925184 and thence via Maen Madoc to join the Ystradfellte to Glyntawe route near Blaen Nedd Isaf Farm at 908144.

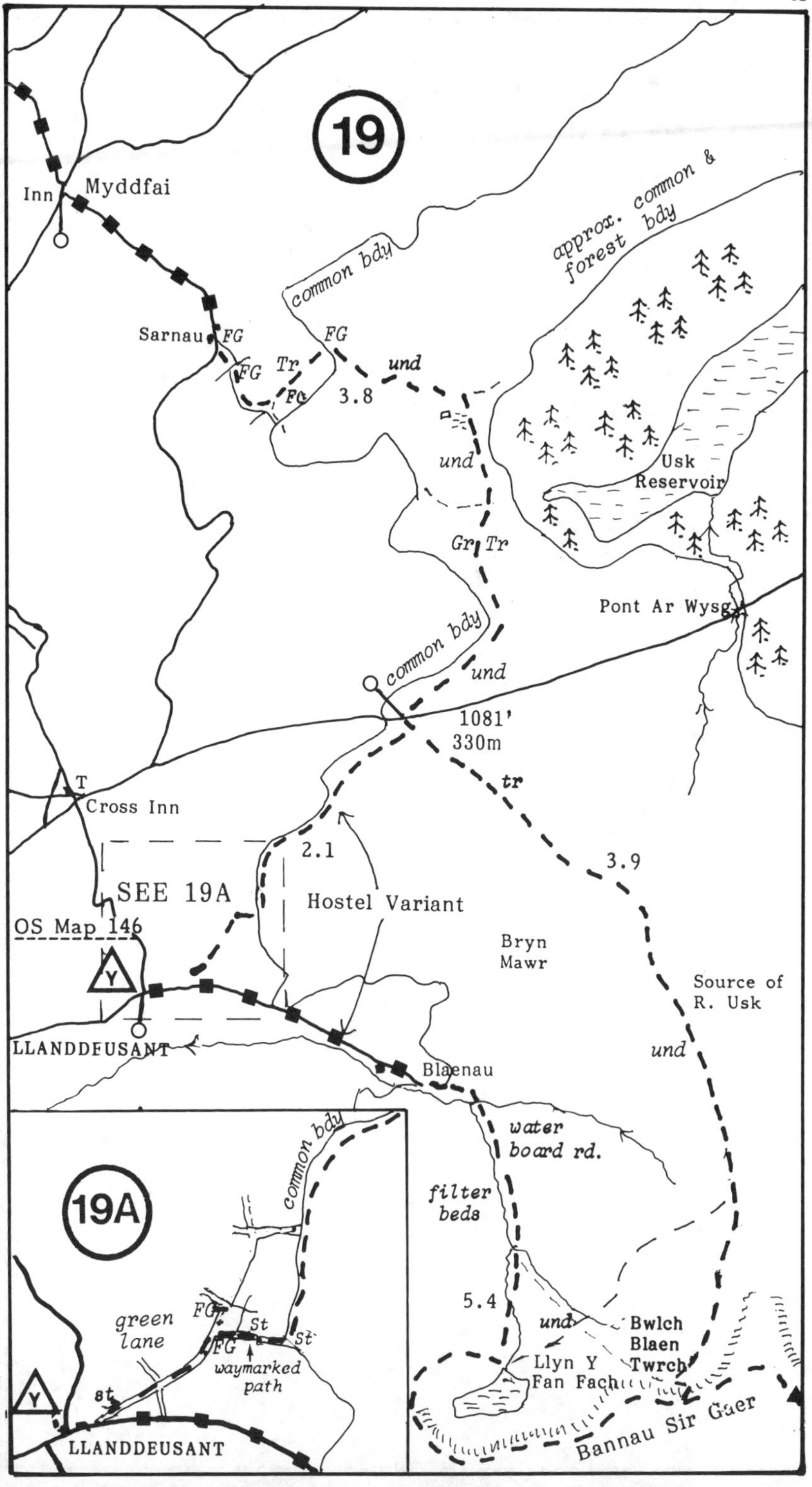

19

Inn Myddfai

common bdy

approx. common & forest bdy

Sarnau *FG* *FG*

FG *Tr* *und*
FG 3.8

Usk Reservoir

und

Gr Tr

Pont Ar Wysg

common bdy *und*

1081'
330m

tr

T
Cross Inn

2.1
Hostel Variant 3.9

SEE 19A

OS Map 146

Bryn
Mawr

Y

Source of
R. Usk

LLANDDEUSANT

und

Blaenau

water
board rd.

filter
beds

19A

common bdy

green
lane *FG* *St*
FG *St*
waymarked
path

Y
St

LLANDDEUSANT

5.4 *und* Bwlch
Blaen
Twrch
Llyn Y
Fan Fach

Bannau Sir Gaer

42

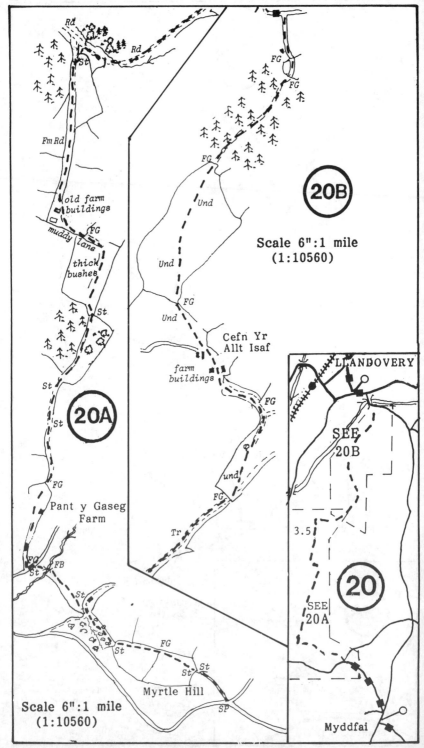

Rd

Rd

St

Fm Rd

old farm
buildings

muddy lane

FG

thick
bushes

St

St

St

20A

St

FG

Pant y Gaseg
Farm

FG

St   FB

St

St

FG

St

St   St

Myrtle Hill

SP

Scale 6":1 mile
(1:10560)

FG

FG

FG

Und

Und

FG

Und

Cefn Yr
Allt Isaf

farm
buildings

FG

und

FG

Tr

20B

Scale 6":1 mile
(1:10560)

LLANDOVERY

SEE
20B

3.5

SEE
20A

20

Myddfai

The Carmarthen Vans (Van = peak). I have always understood the term Carmarthen Vans to refer to the mountain range marked on the maps as the Black Mountain and the western end of Fforest Fawr. The Black Mountain (not to be confused with the Black Mountains at the other end of the national park) is in the former and future county of Carmarthen (Sir Gaer), though meanwhile part of Dyfed county. The Fforest Fawr section was in the county of Brecknock, also known as Breconshire, and now part of Powys county. Both constitute one enormous open moor to which there has been de facto public access from time immemorial. Farms from some distance around have grazing rights on these two commons. The Black Mountain was acquired by the national park authority in 1988 after abortive purchase by an Egyptian who was unable to complete the purchase and then by an unknown buyer.

The highest part of, the mountain range has two principal summits, though neither can really be called peaks in the true sense. Bannau Brycheiniog (Brecknock Peaks) is the highest at 2630 feet / 802 metres, while the next highest is Bannau Sir Gaer at 2460 feet / 750 metres.

The walker may wonder how shepherds find their flocks if the sheep can wander anywhere on such a vast fenceless common. Under the hefting system the sheep get to know their patch and stick to it. They pass on their knowledge to their lambs. Sheep are very lost if driven off their patch and this is one reason why walkers should not have a dog with them. Sheep instinctively run away from a dog, even if it is on a lead. Unless surprised by walkers sheep are generally fairly oblivious to walkers as such and there need be no conflict of interest .

Carmarthen Vans to Llandovery.   Maps 19,19A,20,20A & 20B
From the summits of the Carmarthen Vans the recommended route depends on whether the walker needs a roof for the night. The Youth Hostel in the tiny hamlet of Llanddeusant provides the excuse to walk the top of the superb escarpment of Bannau Sir Gaer, overlooking Llyn y Fan Fach and then to drop down to the lake and follow the water board road down to Blaenau and along a narrow minor road into Llanddeusant. Return route to the common is by grassy lanes.

The main route from Bannau Brycheiniog strikes northwards and continues over open land for another six miles before descending to lower levels with enclosed fields and roads. Avoid the obvious steep and erosion prone nose of Fan Foel and strike westwards to the pass of Bwlch Blaen Twrch at 816218, and down a zig-zag path before heading northwards. Our Mountain Connoisseur is however advised to do the whole circuit of Bannau Sir Gaer and down to Llyn y Fan Fach before contouring round to the direct route. Llyn y Fan Fach is the site of one of the most fascinating of Welsh legends, that of the Lady of the Lake. See Richard Sale's "A Cambrian - Way" and many other books.

The way via the source of the Usk and Bryn Mawr is fairly featureless and expert map and compass work may be necessary. About a mile after crossing the Llanddeusant to Trecastle road the black pecks on the 1:50,000 map do a sharp left turn (802278). Here strike north on an undefined route requiring expert navigation. The common is left by a grass track down to Sarnau and a narrow road followed to the village of Myddfai. Minor road walking is necessary to Myrtle Hill, whence follow little used tracks and paths to Llandovery. The maps 20A and 20B are six inch to the mile and should ensure lack of navigational problems on this very pleasant section which is in such sharp contrast to the stark open landscapes of the Brecon Beacons.

Llandovery is a natural staging and revictualing point. It has ample accommodation, eating houses, a camp site and tourist information office. Hostellers will tend to make it a midday call between Llanddeusant and Bryn Poeth. If the Cambrian Way is being walked in three sections then the rail service to Llandovery will prove useful.

CENTRAL SECTION
Llandovery to Dinas Mawddwy
Via the Elenydd and Plynlimon

Distance 77 6 miles (124.2km)   Ascent 12666 feet (3863m)

After a generally east to west traverse of the Brecon Beacons National Park, our Connoisseur must now set face to the north in earnest. Let it not be thought, however, that the next few days of walking are just a beeline for Snowdonia. For those with a limited knowledge of Wales the central section is likely to be a revelation as to the wildness and beauty that is seen by few visitors to Wales.

The route crosses the Elenydd and Plynlimon ranges, both large and remote areas of mountain and moorland, which though having many crags and outcrops have few spectacular summits. In 1972 the Countryside Commission tried to designate these areas as a national park but there was much opposition locally. Much to the disgust of the Commission, and amenity and tourist interests, the Secretary of State for Wales, without even holding a public inquiry, refused to confirm the designation order. If this area had become a national park 80% of the Cambrian Way would have been in a national park. With hindsight the Commission might have been wiser to have gone for the lower status of an " Area of Outstanding Natural Beauty".

Forestry is the greatest threat to wildlife and amenity interests in this area. The many grants and tax concessions given to commercial tree growing has led to vast areas in the Elenydd being planted with conifers, though rather more on the eastern side than the western. This led Cambrian Way surveyors to suggest a line near the west side of the range, even though this meant omitting the scenic qualities of the Elan Valley reservoirs. In fact only five miles of the route in the central section goes through conifer woodlands.

There are not so many ridges and escarpments to follow in the central section but this is made up for by the attractiveness of the valleys walked, notably the Twyi (Towy), Doethie and Rheiddol.

Llandovery to Rhandirmwyn   6. 6 miles   1033 feet of ascent   Map 21

From Llandovery the next objective is likely to be Rhandirmwyn or Bryn Poeth Uchaf Youth Hostel. The most obvious ridge north of Llandovery has no public access at all so the choice lies between following the Towy valley by footpaths and roads through Cilycwm village or the recommended more direct route following a very minor road on the east side of Fforest ridge, then an untarred old road for 0.8 miles to 783407 (spot ht 219m). *Between there and 784418 follow map 21A. The byway followed was completely omitted from the 1991 OS 160 map (Brecon Beacons) due to Dyfed C.C.mistakenly deleting the byway because it is classified as a road,though mostly grass. It should appear again in the next edition.* At the road reached at 784418 hostellers turn right while main route followers go straight on and down to the Towy itself and follow the river path to Rhandirmwyn.

Rhandirmwyn belies its name, which means "district of mines", for the old lead mines are barely visible in the delectable valley in which this scattered village is situated. There is a large campsite, post office stores (last for 19 miles) and a pub.

This area is very much RSPB country, with many species of birds in the woods of the nature reserves. This is the most likely area on the Cambrian Way to see a kite, a species that nearly became extinct, but which is now much protected and increasing in numbers. The kite is liable to desert its young if disturbed and a year's brood may be lost . Kites do sometimes nest in the Doethie valley which lies ahead and this led to opposition to Cambrian Way going that way, but all the alternatives suggested could have similar objections. The Doethie has a public path along it and is a regular route between the youth hostels of Bryn Poeth and Tyncornel, so seems a reasonable route, which at least avoids the nature reserves.

Side excursions can be made to Dinas nature reserve and the Llyn Brianne but they involve tourist road walking, and return same way if the whole of the Doethie

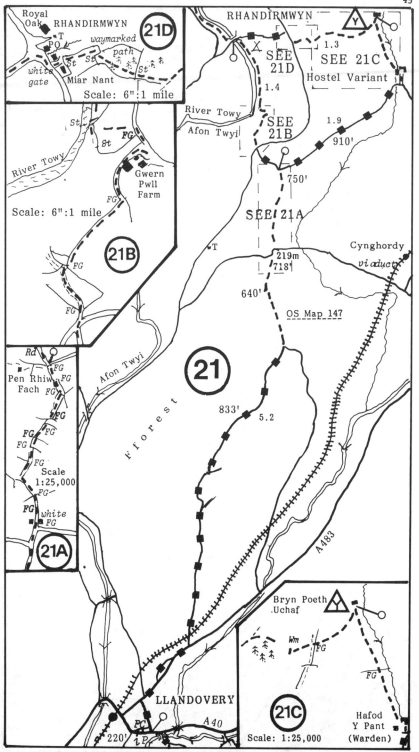

21D

Royal Oak RHANDIRMWYN
PO T
St *waymarked path*
St St
white gate Miar Nant St
Scale: 6":1 mile

21B

St
FG
River Towy St
Gwern Pwll Farm
Scale: 6":1 mile
FG
FG
FG

21A

Rd
FG
Pen Rhiw Fach FG
FG
FG FG
FG
FG
Scale 1:25,000
FG
FG white FG

RHANDIRMWYN
Y
SEE 21D
1.3
SEE 21C
Hostel Variant
1.4
River Towy
Afon Twyi
SEE 21B
1.9
910'
SEE 21A
750'
219m 718'
Cynghordy *viaduct*
T
640'
OS Map 147
21
F f o r e s t
Afon Twyi
833' 5.2
A 483

Bryn Poeth Uchaf

21C

Wm FG
FG
Scale: 1:25,000
Hafod Y Pant (Warden)

LLANDOVERY
PC
220' P A 40

Tyncornel

old road

chapel

Soar Y Mynydd

Dolgoch 2½m

FG

hostel variant

2.1

Nant Llwyd

FG

SEE 22B

22B

FG

FG

Nant Llwyd Farm

1.9

(22)

River Doethie

2.5

Llyn Brianne

Troedrhiw-cymmer

River Pysgotwr

Dam

Allt Rhyd Y Groes National Nature Reserve

Troedrhiw Ruddwen

Gwenffrwd Nature Reserve

Dinas Nature Reserve

3

River Towy

OS Map 160

old track

SP

FG

old river bank

Scale: 6":1 mile

river gets wider near point to turn

22A

follow river edge

TOWY BRIDGE Check Point 15

inn

T

Nantybai

Rhandirmwyn

1.0

SEE 22A

SEE 21D

SEE 21C

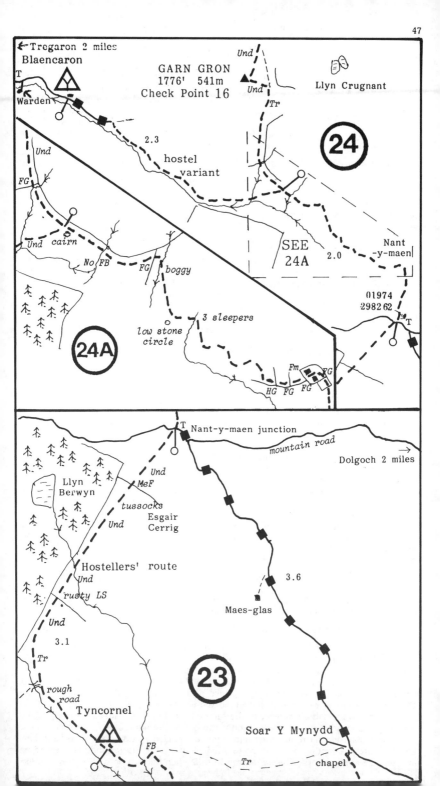

← Tregaron 2 miles
Blaencaron
T
Warden

GARN GRON
1776' 541m
Check Point 16

Llyn Crugnant

(24)

2.3

hostel
variant

Und

FG

Und cairn

No FB   FG   boggy

SEE
24A

2.0

Nant
-y-maen

01974
2982 62

T

3 sleepers

low stone
circle

(24A)

Fm   FG

HG FG FG

T Nant-y-maen junction

mountain road

→
Dolgoch 2 miles

Llyn
Berwyn

Und
MeF
tussocks
Esgair
Cerrig
Und

Hostellers' route

Und

rusty LS

Und

3.1

Tr

rough
road

Tyncornel

3.6

Maes-glas

(23)

FB

Tr

Soar Y Mynydd

chapel

valley is to be walked, as it should be. The Dinas reserve is a densely wooded hill with the rushing Towy on two sides, a circular path round it and a spur up to a cleft known as Twm Shon Catti' s cave, where the Welsh equivalent of Robin Hood lived in hiding. Llyn Brianne is a large holding reservoir built in the early '70s. It is an impressive site but it did drown a very attractive wooded valley. The dam, which the author considers the ugliest imaginable, is excused by Richard Sale as a " thoroughly modern dam " .

Rhandirmwyn to Nant-y-maen   12 miles   1579 feet of ascent   Maps 22&23.

To return to the main route, we now enter the Doethie valley, which in the author's opinion is the most attractive valley on the whole Cambrian Way. The lower part has extensive natural woods on one side and craggy hillside with scattered trees on the other. A particularly delectable spot is the confluence of the Towy and Doethie with attractive waterfalls. The tarred road ends at Troedrhiw Ruddwen farm.Shortly after, a rough road leads off to Troedrhiwcymmer, but the valley path becomes a grass route, sometimes muddy, but always with attractive valley sides and scattered trees. At 771514 non-hostellers must bear right and climb steeply before descent to the remote chapel at Soar y Mynydd (784533) and thence by minor road to the Tregaron- Abergwesyn road near Nant-y-maen (762577). Hostellers will continue up the valley to Tyncornel, the most remote hostel in Wales. Compared with Bryn Poeth it is more accessible inasmuch as you can get a car to it by a long lonely road from Llandewi Brefi, whereas you cannot get a car anywhere near Bryn Poeth. Tyncornel, however, is much more out in the wild. From the hostel road onwards to Nant y Maen, the route is not on the definitive map of rights of way, but there is a long standing arrangement for its use by hostellers .

Nant-y-maen to Strata Florida   6½ miles   946 feet of ascent   Maps 24&25

From the farm at Nant-y-maen careful navigation is necessary as the path is not always visible and both rough ground and streams have to be crossed. The large cairn at 745595 is the junction for Blaencaron Youth Hostel and Tregaron. Garn Gron summit, not far off the faint track, though only 1776 feet is a worthy check point, and gives a good distant view on a clear day both back to the Brecon Beacons and on to Plynlimon. The way continues over wild open country, though with forestry growing up to the east. Around about 738623 the diversion for Pontrhydfendigaid divides from the main route heading for Strata Florida. The latter route,still undefined, crosses a stream and enters new forestry at a gate with white marking and the Cambrian Way hat logo. By arrangement with the Forestry Commission the author has waymarked the bridleway route with blue arrows as far as Talwrn. The way through the dangerous buildings at Talwrn, marked by black dashes on the O.S. map, is said to be a right of way and agreement has been given for its use. Just before reaching the abbey remains at Strata Florida a deep stream has taken over the enclosed footpath and in most seasons the water is well over boot level, so be prepared.

A visit to Pontrhydfendigaid (Bridge at the ford of the Blessed One) may be desirable for replenishing stores and for the bird watcher could be a place for a rest day, with a visit to Tregaron Bog, a national nature reserve nearby. A footpath on the north side of the Teifi returns the walker to the main route at Strata Florida.

Strata Florida to Cwmystwyth   9 miles 1408 feet of ascent   Maps 26 & 27.

The remains of Stratá Florida Abbey are open to the public on payment. The route follows part of the ancient monks' route across wild moorlands to Abbey Cwmhir. This is a road as far as Ty'n-y-cwm. A turn off is made below Llyn Egnant, one of the series of wild lakes known as Teifi Pools. From there nearly to Cwmystwyth one is on land with a public right of access either because it is on Crown common or because it is on land within the gathering grounds of the Elan Valley reservoirs which are subject to the famous Birmingham Clauses (see page 14). There is no defined route acros the moorland to get to Domen Milwyn, our next check point, but Claerddu farm buildings,and three lakes, Llyn Fyrddin Fawr and Fach and Llyn Du provide landmarks. The watershed of the gathering grounds is marked at intervals by stone pillars. The panorama from Domen Milwyn on a clear day is even

49

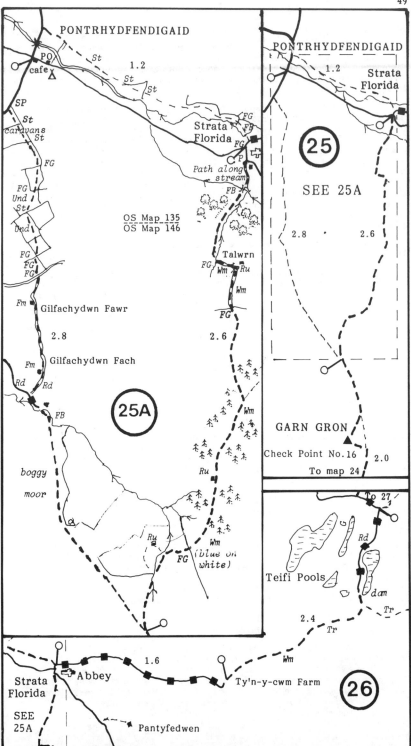

more wild than Garn Gron. From the summit descend NW to a stile,then follow line of dead end footpath marked on map on NE side of Nant Milwyn towards Cwmystwyth . Follow route marked on map 27A into Cwmystwyth unless waymarks and/or amendment sheets to this book dictate otherwise as changes may be made here.

Cwmystwyth was the scene of much lead mining, which was in its heyday at the end of the 19th century. Enormous mine buildings, closed in 1921, are situated one mile up the valley from the village and stand as a monstrous eyesore or gaunt industrial relic according to taste. Those with time to spare can keep north from Domen Milwyn and ford the Ystwyth to visit the ruins but beware - the buildings are very dangerous. See Simon Hughes "The Cwmystwyth Mine" (published by Northern Mine Research Society) . The river below the mine has incidentally been irrevocably polluted by water from the mine. The village itself has attractive surroundings. Donald Hoare, who was the project officer appointed by the Countryside Commission to report on the central section of the Cambrian Way (see page 7) lives in Cwmystwyth and is willing to advise walkers and hear of any problems they have encountered . He can be contacted at the Old School (see map) .

Cwmystwyth to Dyffryn Castell   via Devil's Bridge and Ponterwyd
10½ miles   1930 feet of ascent   Maps 28 & 29

From the Cwmystwyth area it is possible to make a beeline for Plynlimon by going via Llethr Nant-Hylles or Myherin Forest and crossing the A44 at Eisteddfa Gurig or Dyffryn Castell, but this route would omit the spectacular Rheidol gorge and the fascinating areas of Devil's Bridge and Ystumtuen. As it requires considerable extra effort to follow the recommended route via the Rheidol valley the author has nominated Pontbren Plwca, the bridge over the Rheidol at 727782, as a checkpoint for achievement of his version of the Cambrian Way.

For the Rheidol route leave Cwmystwyth by gate opposite the old school and follow the map closely on some ill-defined paths to Forestry Commission forest and thence to The Arch, a stone structure over the Cwmystwyth to Devil's Bridge road built in 1810 to commemorate George III's accession. A pleasant track commencing shortly to west of the arch leads to Devil's Bridge avoiding the sometimes busy tourist road .

Devil's Bridge (Pontarfrynach) is a somewhat congested tourist honeypot at the end of a narrow gauge railway. It is nevertheless worth a visit if only to see the three generations of bridges, one above the other, the oldest being 900 years old. The splendour of the Mynach Falls, which you have to pay to see, varies, of course, according to the amount of water flowing. The footpath off the A4120 leads to the railway track but do not cross it yet. 300 metres on cross line into nature reserve then cross back again 110 metres on, near a waterfall. .At time of writing the right of way is then alongside railway track itself but a legal diversion on the upper side has been imminent for some time (see29A). The diverted route doubles back to the original path which descends to footbridge called Pontbren Plwca (check point 18). This superb spot, with waterfalls and the beautiful Rheidol valley around, was once marred by the Cwm Rheidol lead mine, relics of which are passed on the waymarked path up to Ystumtuen. See Youth Hostel section for information about Ystumtuen. The route continues to Dyffryn Castell using a short stretch of the A44 at Ponterwyd and passing a post office/shop. An alternative is to follow a waymarked route to Parson's Bridge, a recently replaced footbridge over a really dramatic and deep gorge, but the rest of the way involves 2½ miles of road walking.

Dyffryn Castell to Dylife via Plynlimon (Punlumon)
11½- miles   2560 feet of ascent   Maps 30 31

The approach to Plynlimon from Dyffryn Castell is long and relatively little used compared to the shorter route from Eisteddfa Gurig. Much of the way is undefined and in cloud a compass will be necessary until the fence is reached, after which one is by a fence almost to the summit. There one will find a ring of stones in which many walkers have sought shelter from wind and rain. Here on the main summit of Plynlimon one can really feel one is at the heart of Wildest Wales.

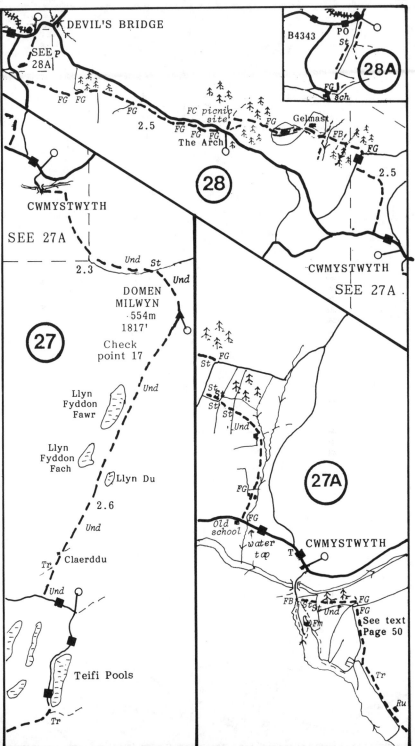

29

A 44

Mining museum

Llywernog

PONTERWYD

PCt

SEE 1.8

29C

A 44

Dyffryn Castell Hotel

SEE 29B

1.9

Parson's Bridge

Wm

FB

3.9

A 4120

George Borrow Hotel

FG

FB

St St

St

29B

Check Point 18
PONTBREN PLWCA

△

Ystumtuen

Wm

0.7

200' 61m

1.1

SEE 29A

Afon Rheidol

A 4120

DEVIL'S BRIDGE

29C

A 44

P.O. Shop

KG KG

FG

PONTERWYD

Ystumtuen

St

St

warden
Youth Hostel
chapel

0.7

St

Tr

Und

St

disused mine

Fm

FB

KG

Rhiwfron Halt

St

Afon Rheidol

1.1

Tr

Mynach Falls

29A

A 4120

FG

und

hotel

DEVIL'S BRIDGE

PO

P

Plynlimon is Crown common with a legal right of public access (see page 14) but this right was under threat in 1983 due to a misguided scheme of the Crown Estate Commissioners, following buying up of the last remaining commoner, to fence off certain areas to provide shelter belts for tree planting and to improve other areas. The scheme was to be in commemoration of the marriage of the Prince and Princess of Wales but this gesture was not at all appreciated by the Countryside Commission or any of the amenity bodies such as the Ramblers' Association, Council for the Protection of Rural Wales and the Youth Hostels Association. They were particularly incensed that the Crown Estate erected a long barbed wire fence before the Secretary of State for the Environment had had a chance to decide if it was for the "benefit of the neighbourhood ". In the event the Secretary of State settled for a compromise so that no new fences appear near the summit but the prematurely erected fence (not seen from Cambrian Way) has periodic stiles in it.

The Machynlleth Variant. The summit of Plynlimon is a possible junction for beeliners determined to get to Cader Idris via Machynlleth. This saves 16 miles compared with the recommended route. There is a fine route on rights of way via Hyddgen, the escarpment of Creigiau Bwlch Hyddgen and passing east of Glanmerin Lake to Machynlleth. This busy little market town may prove an attraction with its better supplies than those available from the village post offices recently encountered. Looking ahead on the main route in this guide one can expect good grocery shops at Mallwyd and Dinas Mawddwy and then not until Barmouth. Beyond Machynlleth there are routes into a much forested area but except for the A487 through Corris there is no right of way into the Talyllyn valley to the SE of Cader Idris between the way to Abergynolwyn via Foel y Geifr and the footpath to Bwlch Lynn Bach from Cwm Ratgoed. The Abergynolwyn approach to Cader Idris is long and involving a repeat of the top section on the descent, and is not nearly such a good way up as the two offered in this guide. The road route from Corris is preceeded by more road walking from Machynlleth, although the Centre for Alternative Technology can be visited on the way. It is because of these problems but rather more the scenic qualities and interest of the route via Dylife, Mynydd Cemmaes, Dinas Mawddwy and the Maesglasau ridge that the Connoisseur is advised to stick to the route in this guide.

Plynlimon has several summits and several sources of famous rivers. The Wye source lies a mile away to the east but more on the route is the source of the Severn. Do not be deceived however by the mobile post indicating the source of the Severn which moves around the boggy area whence floweth the longest river in the British Isles. Go north and cross the valley to hit the track leading round a headland to bring Lake Bugeilyn into view. Follow the bridleway between the two parts of the lake and at the ruins of the Bugeilyn farm cross the stream and go over the bank on an undefined public footpath. Watch for the site of an old reservoir which served the disused mine beyond. Follow the map into Dylife.

Glyndwr's Way. Half a mile before Dylife there is a crossing with a long distance footpath route devised and waymarked by Powys County Council. Glyndwr's Way is in two sections, each crossing from the Welsh coast at Machynlleth to the Offa's Dyke Path along the border with England. This is the southern section to Knighton. The northern section to Welshpool will be crossed near Commins Coch.

Glyndwr's Way is being considered for full national trail status by the Countryside Council for Wales. It traverses quiet and attractive Welsh countryside but the route as devised by Powys C.C.has 36 of its 120 miles along tarred roads, i.e. 30% compared to 11% for Cambrian Way. In particular, it currently follows 3 miles of the busy A489 from Machynlleth. Unless dramatically improved, properly waymarked, and many miles of new rights of way created it is unlikely to appeal greatly to our Mountain Connoiseur.

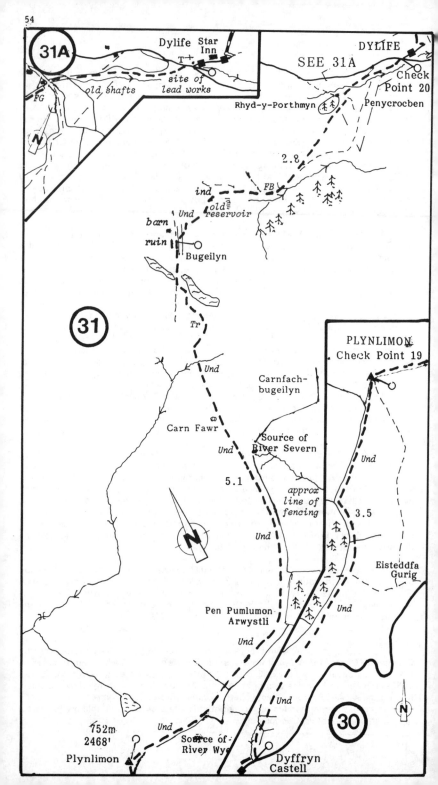

31A

Dylife Star Inn

DYLIFE

SEE 31A

T

site of
lead works

Check
Point 20

FG

old shafts

Rhyd-y-Porthmyn

Penycrocben

N

2.8

ind

FB

Und

old
reservoir

barn

ruin

Bugeilyn

31

Tr

Und

PLYNLIMON
Check Point 19

Carnfach-
bugeilyn

Carn Fawr

Source of
River Severn

Und

Und

5.1

approx
line of
fencing

3.5

Und

N

Eisteddfa
Gurig

Und

Pen Pumlumon
Arwystli

Und

Und

30

N

Und

752m
2468'

Plynlimon

Und

Source of
River Wye

Dyffryn
Castell

Dylife. It is hard to believe that this quiet hamlet, 1200 feet up in the hills, with only a few houses and a pub, was, just over a century ago, the scene of intense mining activity. At that time vast quantities of lead were being mined, also copper and zinc, and many hundreds of miners were employed. The Romans almost certainly mined here and there was a fortlet on Penycrocbren, the hill to the south. It is a ghostly place with bare areas where the mine buildings have been removed and a churchyard with tombstones but no church left. The derelict barrack buildings are a reminder of the overcrowding that went on here with one bed shared by two miners who each did a 12-hour shift, and got into the warm bed left by the other. Pencrocbren (meaning gallows hill) has a gruesome tale to tell of a blacksmith at the mine who murdered his wife and daughter and threw their bodies down a disused shaft. At that time it was the custom to hang murderers near the scene of their crirne and for the body to hang in a metal cage. His last job was to make his own cage, which is still preserved at St. Fagans Folk museum at Cardiff.

The Star Inn is partly very old, with modern additions for a restaurant and bedrooms. If time permits a stroll should be made down the road from the village until the rnagnificent view down into the Pennant valley is obtained with the crags on the left and the waterfall of Ffrwd Fawr. For further reading see " Dylife" written and published by David Bick, Pound House, Newent, Glos. (1985 edition £2.10 post free).

Dylife to Conmins Coch 8½ miles   750 feet of ascent   Map 32

The next section of the Cambrian Way is in complete contrast to the starkness of Plynlimon. It is a fascinating undulating walk over two attractive passes, with a mixture of rough and improved grassland, forest and heather moorland. The whole route is shown at 1:25,000 scale as well as 1:50,000 because many field boundaries have to be crossed and it is necessary to have maps showing relevant boundaries to help the walker to keep to public rights of way. Paths are less used in these parts and some minor diversions are necessary where paths are obstructed but hopefully these will be dealt with by Powys C.C..

In the woods west of Esgair Geulan follow the paths and forest roads as shown on the map. Part of the right of way was planted on but a legal diversion between 848975 and 849979 was stimulated by the author and became operative in July 1984, and is waymarked. At Maesteg the Forestry Commission allows the use of the forest road but watch for the public footpath which turns sharply down at a bend in the forest road. (See page 15)

Commins Coch is a small village with a post office/shop but no pub Trains pass through but do not stop nearer than Machynlleth to the west and Caersws to the east. There is a pleasant spot for a picnic on common land alongside the rushing river Twymyn to the south-east of the village at 849029. The nearest B&B is 377 up to a magnificent viewpoint at Cefn Coch Uchaf, or you can press on to "Gwalia". A path route for diversion to Cemmaes is shown as map 33B but at the time of writing there is no B&B there (watch amendment sheets).

Commins Coch to Dinas Mawddwy 13 miles 2460 feet of ascent   Map 33

Mynydd y Cemmaes is a broad ridge of some 2½ miles length giving fine views of the surrounding valleys and of Snowdonia's principal summits. Until 1992 It was a quiet and wild place with little sign of the bridleways to be followed on the Cambrian Way route. Now there is a line of 24 wind generators along the ridge, constituting the first windfarm in Wales. The author protested at the public inquiry in support of the Countryside Council for Wales and many amenity bodies, putting the view that the visual effect and fears of the precedent created for other parts of the Cambrian Way was not justified for the relatively small amount of "green" power to be produced. Our Mountain Connoisseur will either be horrified or fascinated, but should be warned not to go too close in a gale, as blades have been known to come off when the power supply line came down which operates the mechanism to turn the turbines off and face the wind.

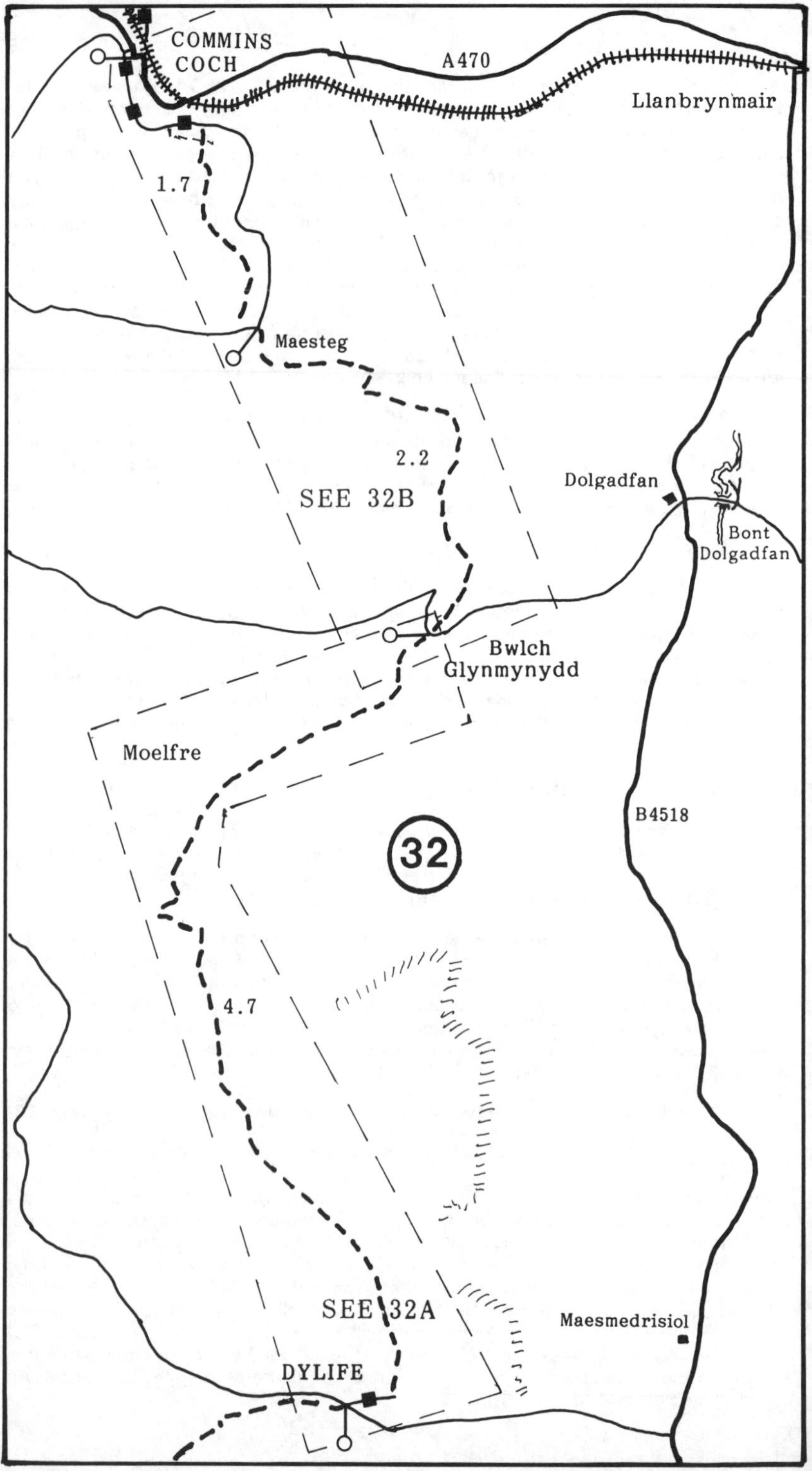

COMMINS COCH

A470

Llanbrynmair

1.7

Maesteg

2.2

SEE 32B

Dolgadfan

Bont Dolgadfan

Bwlch Glynmynydd

Moelfre

(32)

B4518

4.7

SEE 32A

Maesmedrisiol

DYLIFE

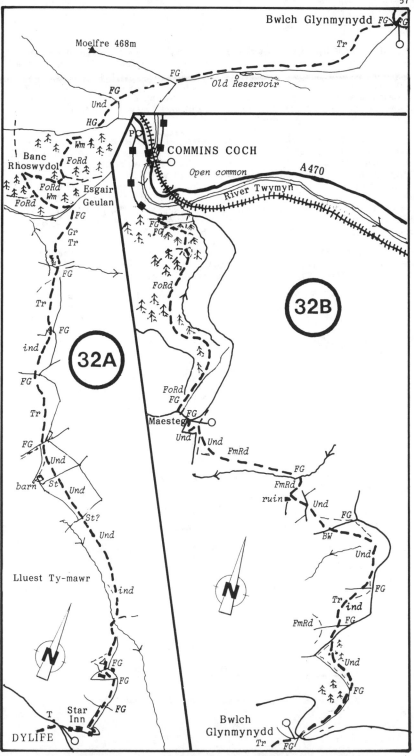

North of Mynydd Cemmaes the only route zig zags somewhat via Waun Llinau and Esgair Ddu into the Tafalog valley and thence by stony road to Mallwyd. On the experimental 124 Landranger map, due July 1995, this latter road is to be marked with open red diamonds (see pages 13/14) . Mallwyd has a supermarket and the Brigands Inn,which only has a restaurant licence. The minor road suggested to Dinas Mawddwy passes a delectable spot by the Dyfi (Dovey) river at Pont Mallwyd and is preferable to the busy main road.

Dinas Mawddwy with its majestic setting at the junction of the Dovey and Cerist rivers will prove a worthy place to stay for the sheer beauty of its surroundings. Dinas Mawwdwy was once noted for the lawlessness of its red headed brigands. It is diifficult to imagine how this village was once an important borough and market town. A century ago slate mining was the thriving industry but the railway that was built to serve it closed in 1951. The former railway station is now a cafe attached to the woollen and craft enterprise and shop. On sale is a fascinating booklet on the history of Dinas Mawddwy. Be sure to look over the now bypassed road bridge to see a much older packhorse bridge.

The camp site,Celyn Brithion, has a superb panoramic spot for backpackers on rising ground above the caravan section. The Red Lion (Llew Coch) is the older of the two inns and Welsh singing with organ is assured on Saturday nights.

From Dinas Mawddwy a side excursion can be made to the **Arans**. Although never part of the author's route for the Cambrian Way, they are fine mountains and slightly higher than Cader Idris. The row over access seems to have died down but whereas there used to be open access the way is now more confined with fences and ladder stiles. Road walking is involved to and from Cwm Cywarch. Distance 12½ miles and 3000ft of ascent

END OF CENTRAL SECTION

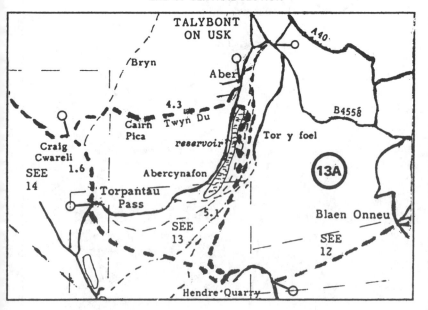

Map showing the **Talybont Variant** (see page 33)

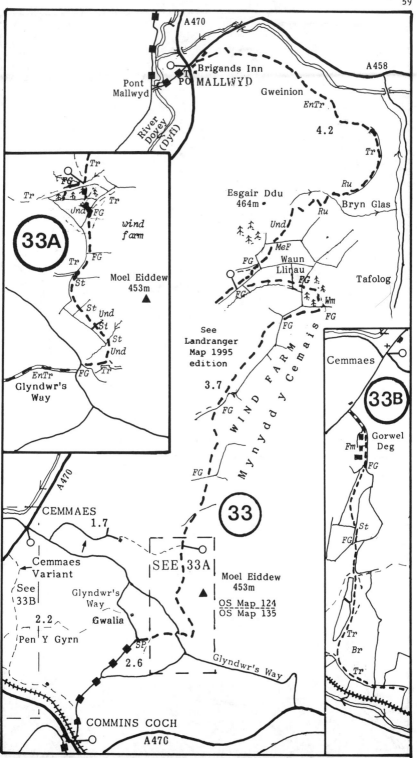

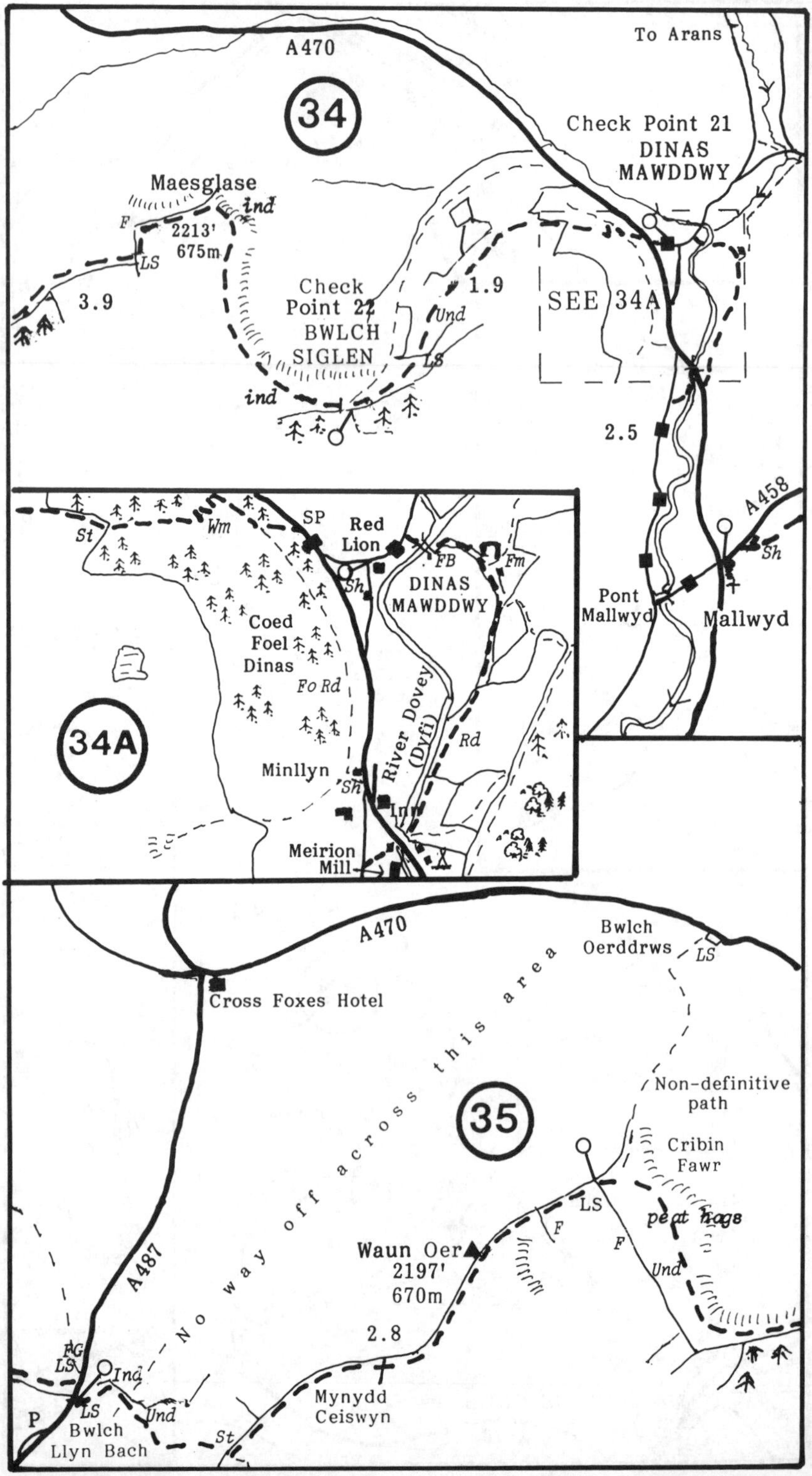

Map 34

A470

To Arans

Check Point 21
DINAS MAWDDWY

Maesglase
ind
F
2213'
675m
LS

3.9

Check Point 22
BWLCH SIGLEN

1.9
Und
LS

SEE 34A

ind

2.5

A458

Pont Mallwyd

Mallwyd

Sh

Map 34A

St
Wm
SP
Red Lion
Sh
FB
Fm

DINAS MAWDDWY

Coed Foel Dinas

Fo Rd

River Dovey (Dyfi)

Rd

Minllyn
Sh
In

Meirion Mill

Map 35

A470

Cross Foxes Hotel

Bwlch Oerddrws
LS

Non-definitive path

Cribin Fawr

No way off across this area

35

peat hags

A487

LS

F
F
Und

Waun Oer
2197'
670m

2.8

AG
LS
Ind
P
LS
Und

Bwlch Llyn Bach

St

Mynydd Ceiswyn

NORTHERN SECTION
Dinas Mawddwy to Conwy
Through Snowdonia National Park

88.1 miles (141.8 km)   27,711 ft ascent (8452m)

Dinas Mawddwy to Barmouth via Maesglase,Waun-oer and Cader Idris
20 miles   5526 feet of ascent   Maps 34 to 38

Part of the obliquely ascending path through the forest of Coed Foel Dinas has been diverted, necessitating a detour along a forest road and then a steep zig zag climb back to the line of the original right of way. The author originally complained in 1979 about the obstruction caused by a cliff formed when the forest road was made, It took from 1984 to 1995 for Gwynedd County Council to process a proper diversion, no less than 26 letters being sent by the author over the period. Beyond the diversion the rough and gradually ascending path gets steeper before emerging onto the open hillside at a corner of the moor.

Bwlch Siglen to Mynydd Ceiswyn via Maesglase and Waun Oer is one of the finest sections of Cambrian Way with superb crag top walking ,wild moorland and superb views. Between Bwlch Siglen and Cribin Fawr the route is across public access land provided under a Tir Cymen agreement (see page 15) and is mostly clearly defined on the ground with ladder stiles at fences. A short peaty section on Cribin Fawr is best passed on the north side. The fine ridge walking continues south-westwards and is eroded on the steep approach to Waun-oer.

Bwlch Llyn Bach is presumably the name of the pass on the A487 despite its marking on the Ordnance maps on the opposite side of a filled-in lake which gives its name to the pass (now a lay-by). Here a decision has to be made as to alternatives. The main route makes the approach to Cader Idris involving the least ascent. From a ladder stile off the road on the north side of the pass, follow up a well worn path by a fence for about a mile before a steeper scramble onto the broad main ridge of the mountain. If using the Cader double sided Leisure map 23,be advised to turn over in a secluded spot and not when the one side runs out on the top of Cader Idris.

The alternative route, involving descent, partly by old road, to the area of Minffordd and Lake Talyllyn, enables a night to be spent there before making the most exciting approach to Cader Idris. This involves a steep wooded ascent by cascading waterfalls followed by a spectacular ridge climb, marked as the Minffordd Path, round the enormous cwm surrounding Llyn Cau..

On the writer's first visit to Cader Idris a man in a little hut on the summit dispensed cups of tea but there is no such hospitality there today to greet the many who climb this deservedly popular mountain. Perhaps more practically useful on occasions is the emergency shelter just to the north of the summit. The whole mountain is a national nature reserve.

It is tempting to descend by Fox's Path but this is very steep, terribly eroded and strongly advised against. Much the better route is westwards by gradual descent to the Pony Path at Rhiw Gwredydd, thence north-east down a maintained path. Half way down, (unless making for the national park car park), go left through gate, before a hunting gate on main path, and follow less used right of way down to the road.

Hostellers may make a beeline for Kings but they must also be planning ahead and decide whether to press on to Barmouth. Few will be capable of reaching Llanbedr and certainly not Ffestiniog along the Cambrian Way route in one day from Kings. Maybe an easy 5½ mile day to Barmouth with an indulgence in candyfloss and sea bathing is called for before tackling the Rhinogs.

The walk to Barmouth through the lower foothills of Cader, past the Cregennen Lakes and a waymarked path route, partly non-definitive, leading down past Arthog waterfalls to the Mawddach estuary is a fascinating walk. Lovers of walking old railway routes could, as an alternative, follow the beautiful wooded valley down from Kings to the Mawddach estuary and follow the scenic cycle route to Arthog.

FG LS LS
Bwlch
Llyn
Bach
3.1 St

shelter FG
2.2
A487
CADER IDRIS
Check Point 23 ⊙ 36
LS Llyn Cau
2.8

△
P
△ Minffordd
Kings Dol Einion

hostel
variant Afon
Mawddach Fegla
Fach

SEE
37A 0.9 Fegla
Fawr ⊙ 38A LS

⊙ 37 High tide
alternative Path on old railway
HG HG
Rhiw
Gwredydd Pony track 2.4 Arthog
Morfa Mawddach
Station
P

Kings SP
SP

hostel
variant Wm Arthog
Waterfalls ⊙ 38B PC
P
St SP
St FG SP NT SP
⊙ 37A FG Wm
St St
PC LS FB SP FG
Fm P Wm SP
Ty'n-y- T
ceunant FG
FG

Barmouth ⊙ 38 2.1
Bridge
2.2
SEE 38A SP 2.3
△ Cregennen FG
SEE Fm
Arthog 38B Lakes LS
1.3

Barmouth Bridge carries both the Cambrian Coast railway line and a footbridge, for which there is a small toll. The future of the bridge and of the whole line was in some ieoardv in 1980 when it was thought the Teredo beetle was destroying the bridge timbers,but the damage was not as bad as was thought.

Barmouth to Maentwrog or Ffestiniog via the Rhinogs

22½ miles   7928 feet of Ascent   Maps 39 to 41

Barmouth is a fascinating seaside resort sandwiched between the cliffs and either the sea or the Mawddach estuary. Depart by a path which starts as a steep flight of steps alongside an enormous gash of an old quarry. Good navigation is required up to the radio mast and Bwlch y Llan. Thence follows a superb ridge walk that would have been impossible but for negotiation by the national park with the owner for a permissive route with ladder stiles over the high walls The action of the owners is much appreciated but it should be noted that to emphasise that the route is not a public right of way, it is closed on February 5th each year. February is an unlikely and highly dangerous time of year to make an expedition along the Cambrian Way, but an alternative " February 5th Route" is shown on map 39. ·

The Rhinog section of the Cambrian Way is at the same time the most demanding, the most rewarding and the most controversial part of the whole route. The traverse of the range should not be undertaken unless the walker is capable of moving safely over difficult terrain and capable of easy climbing with a pack on., Good navigational ability is essential and **one must be prepared to take much longer than the distances suggest will be necessary.**

Going is reasonably easy as far as the summit of Y Llethr the highest point in the range, but the central and northern sections involve much rock scrambling, often where heather obscures the boulders below. Lone walkers particularly must appreciate the dangers of a sprained ankle or other accident in places where no one will hear or see them. The local volunteer mountain rescue organisation was very apprehensive of the creation of the Cambrian Way, not least because of the difficulty of finding an injured person amongst the rocks.

Very few walkers will be capable of doing the whole range in one day and many will find even half the way more than enough for one day. Those who want a roof over their head will find there is no accommodation near either Cwm Nantcol or Cwm Bychan. A Youth Hostel was opened at Gerddi Bluog with the help of the Countryside Commission, with Cambrian Way in mind and before the project foundered, but it was neither very near the route or easily accessible from the coast road and was closed.The backpacker scores on this part of the route in being able to stay in the mountains.

Stage planning for the normal distance walker, if not camping, or being car assisted from road heads at Cwm Nantcol or Cwm Bychan, is likely to involve a detour to Llanbedr or Harlech. The stage planning chart gives distances involved for a taxi assisted detour and return. For a two day Rhinogs schedule descent is made from the route at Bwlch Drws Ardudwy and Cwm Nantcol followed to Llanbedr or a taxi phoned for from the call box at 623262. Return next day by taxi could be to Maes-y-Garnedd . (See accommodation list for taxi details). For a three day schedule, descent to Cwm Nantcol can be made from Crib y rhiw down gentle slopes on Tir Cymen access land to a gate at 636246,and thence by gated path to the Cwm Nantcol road at 630257, returning to Crib y rhiw same way following day. Cwm Bychan has no convenient phone box for taxi calling but one could do this section in reverse to use the Nantcol phonebox again.This is one part of Cambrian Way where a mobile phone would be useful.

Exhilerating ridge walking along Crib-y-rhiw leads to Y Llethr the highest point on the range. Beyond the summit keep to the end of the plateau and descend down a gully. Do not be tempted by a much eroded steep descent which leads more directly to Llyn Hywel. Rhinog Fach is suggested as a spur route using the scramble up the south end and same route for return to avoid steep and erosion prone descents elsewhere off the mountain.

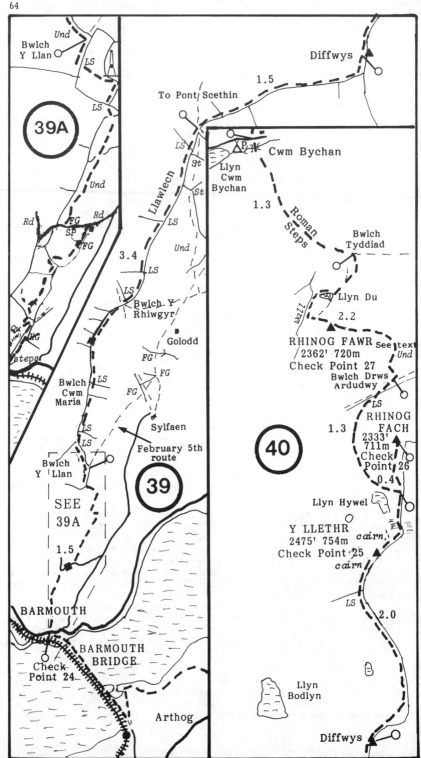

Rhinog Fawr is, next to Tryfan, probably the rockiest mountain in Wales. Geologically and ecologically, however, it is very different, which is no doubt partly why the Nature Conservancy acquired it. Finding the best of many possible routes can be the most difficult piece of navigation on the whole route. Do not be deceived by the wide gradually ascending ledges as seen from the south side, but start scrambling up from just beyond the wall at the actual pass of Bwlch Drws Ardudwy and climb steeply and slightly right, aiming for a small vulnerable cairn on the skyline. Beyond the cairn,if it still exists and you find it, the gradient eases off and one is on a broad rock terrace. Strike half right for a way up the cliff ahead onto one of the more definite paths that lead to the summit.

Descent north-westwards is eroded but unavoidable. Avoid direct descent to Llyn Du and make for wall, then follow wall and north side of lake. North-east from the lake a path leads round to Bwlch Tyddiad but avoid spurious path to left which would take you too high.

The so-called Roman Steps are now agreed as being of later origin. The ready supply of large boulders were used to make a packhorse route over these inhospitable mountains. They now provide thousands of tourists much pleasure and Cambrian Way walkers welcome faster progress than may have been experienced on the Rhinogs. The national park has carried out much improvement to the Steps path with the assistance of working parties of the B.T.C.V. An alternative to the Steps path is to press on along the main ridge via Craig Wion, but the going is very slow and probably not worth the saving of height against the drop to Cwm Bychan.

Cwm Bychan is a grand spot surrounded by rocky mountains and with a most attractive lake. The camp site has no facilities and is seldom crowded in consequence, but this may change if public toilets are erected to cater for the many who park there by day.

The northern Rhinogs are more rocky but less heathery than the central section. From just north of Clip to just west of Moel y Gyrafolen (535m) there is a public right of access because it is a Welsh Crown common . The approach to Clip, and Moel y Gyrafolen are currently permissive access under a Tir Cymen agreement. A steep scramble from just before Bwlch Gwylim is probably the easiest way up to Clip, but it is undefined. Thence follows a remarkable walk, mostly along a bare rock plateau, interspersed with chasms that have to be climbed down and up again. Easy climbing is needed up a rock face but can be circumvented round the sides if necessary. Two small lakes should be identified for help in navigation, especially if the area is in cloud. In contrast Moel Ysgyfarnogod is a grassy mound followed by another dip and cliff to the even flatter rock plateau of Diffwys (not to be confused with the Diffwys at the southern end of the Rhinogs) . It is important to come off the open land by the public footpath at the hunting gate at 674358 to the north of Moel y Gyrafolen. Any other ways in that area would involve climbing over walls, something our Connoisseur never does.

At the minor road at Moelfryn main route walkers will go north by the signposted and waymarked path to the new Trawsfynydd dam and down to Gellilydan and Maentwrog. Those making for Ffestiniog have a choice as to which way they go round Llyn Trawsfynydd. The distance is the same either way. The way round the west and north sides enables one to assess whether Sir Basil Spence and Sylvia 'Crowe made a good job of designing -the nuclear power station and a visitor centre can be a port of call, but if it is desired to keep as far away as possible from anything nuclear then the south and eastern route should be taken. The lake, incidentally,was made to supply hydro electric power in the 1930s and not for the nuclear power station. The Ffestiniog variant was originally intended for hostellers but the hostel was closed in 1995. The variant has been left in as it is attractive.

The alternative routes converge at a Roman amphitheatre now only grassy mounds, with nearby Tomen-y-mur, a Roman fort which Richard Sale describes as "the very frontier of the Empire with pouring rain and pagan savages for company". Waymarked paths lead on to Ffestiniog.

MAENTWROG

Gellilydan

2.3

.A 470

SEE 42A

Roman
Amphitheatre

Hostel
variant

2.2

Nuclear
Power
Station

Nature
Trail

SEE
41B

Llyn Trawsfynydd

1.7

Wm

Trawsfynydd

41A

FG   FG   FG SP

HG

SEE 41A   MOELFRYN
Check Point 29

2.0

St

2.4   Moel Y
Gyrafolen

Diffwys

Und

41

Foel Penolau

MOEL YSGYFARNOGOD
2044' 623m
Check Point 28

Und

2.1

Clip
1937'
Und

Bwych
Gwylim

Wm

FG   Cwm
Bychan

N

Bryn
Tirion   FG

FG

LS   LS

Electric
Power Lines   St pylon

41B

N

New dam

LS

Tr

Tr

dam

approx. boundary

FG

Und   fenced
leat

Llyn
Trawsfynydd

Und   approx. lake bdy

LS

Wm

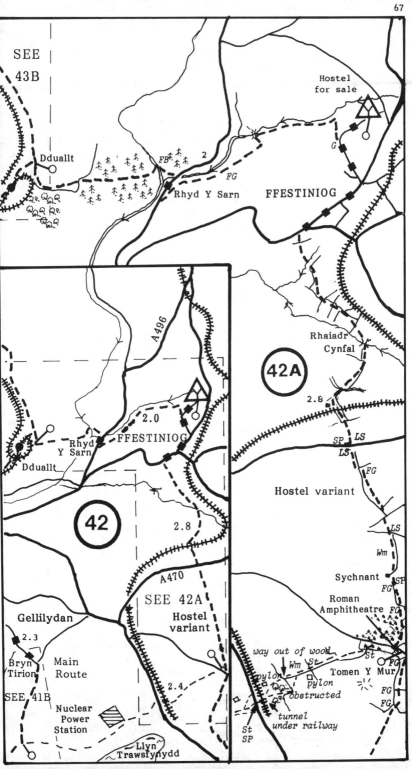

SEE
43B

Hostel
for sale

Dduallt

FB

2

FG

Rhyd Y Sarn   FFESTINIOG

G

A 496

Rhaiadr
Cynfal

42A

2.0

FFESTINIOG

Rhyd
Y Sarn

Dduallt

2.8

SP   LS
LS

FG

Hostel variant

LS

Wm

Sychnant   SP

FG

Roman
Amphitheatre   FG

42

2.8

A 470

SEE 42A

Hostel
variant

2.4

Gellilydan

2.3

Bryn
Tirion

Main
Route

SEE 41B

Nuclear
Power
Station

Llyn
Trawsfynydd

way out of wood

Wm   St

pylon   pylon
            obstructed

tunnel
under railway

St
SP

St   FG

Tomen Y Mur

FG

FG

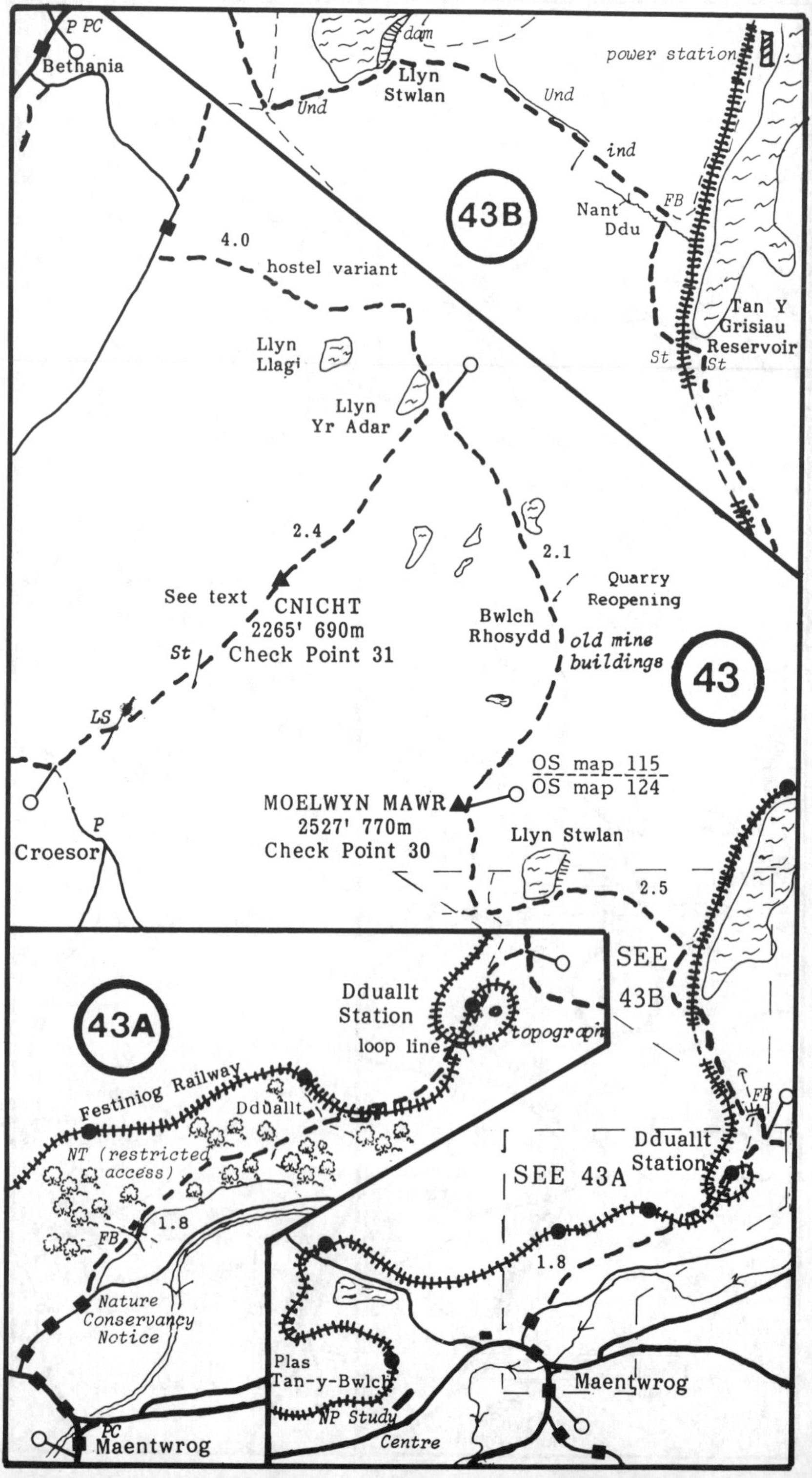

P PC
Bethania

dam
Llyn
Stwlan
Und
Und
ind
power station

43B

Nant
Ddu
FB

4.0   hostel variant

Llyn
Llagi

Llyn
Yr Adar

Tan Y
Grisiau
Reservoir
St   St

2.4

See text
CNICHT
2265' 690m
Check Point 31
St

LS

2.1

Quarry
Reopening

Bwlch
Rhosydd   old mine
buildings

43

Croesor
P

MOELWYN MAWR
2527' 770m
Check Point 30

Llyn Stwlan

OS map 115
OS map 124

2.5

43A

Dduallt
Station
loop line

SEE
43B

topograph

Festiniog Railway   Dduallt
NT (restricted
access)
FB   1.8

Nature
Conservancy
Notice

SEE 43A

Dduallt
Station
FB

1.8

Plas
Tan-y-Bwlch
NP Study
Centre

Maentwrog

PC
Maentwrog

Maentwrog or Ffestiniog to Beddgelert or Bryn Gwynant via Moelwyn Mawr and Cnicht   12. 8 miles   3617 feet of ascent
(Via Ffestiniog and Bryn Gwynant 10.2 miles 3387 feet of ascent)   Maps 42-45.

From Maentwrog a path leads through beautiful woods forming part of the Coed Maentwrog national nature reserve. The National Trust allows restricted access and one is asked to keep to the paths. Our particular path leads round the lower side of a house called Bronturnoruchaf, and thence up to a crossing of the Festiniog railway, which is crossed again at Dduallt station. Due to submergence of part of the disused line when the Tan-y-grisiau reservoir was made, the enterprising organisation seeking to reopen this unique narrow gauge railway had to make a new route at a higher level, involving a new tunnel and the loop under which you pass before reaching the station. The train could be used by Cambrian Way walkers seeking bed and breakfast in Portmadoc or Blaenau Ffestiniog. Beyond the station the path runs a short distance away on the east side of the railway.

Those using the Ffestiniog variant descend by a cascading Afon Teigl to Rhyd-y-sarn and then over the Afon Goedol and through a conifer plantation to rejoin the main route below Dduallt station.

The right of way previously passing across the south end of Tan-y-grisiau reservoir has been diverted to the west side of the railway and should be followed to a footbridge over Nant Ddu, before striking up to Llyn Stwlan on a none too obvious footpath. At the dam go round the south end.

Llyn Stwlan is the upper reservoir of a pump storage system built to enable power from Trawsfynydd nuclear power station to be used at night to pump water from Tan-y-grisiau reservoir up to Llyn Stwlan, then let out to generate power at peak times. At this point and for the way up and down Moelwn Mawr the question of following a right of way is rather academic since there is public right of access because it is either crown common or a common in the former urban district of Ffestiniog .

Moelwyn Mawr is a worthy summit with fine views (if clear of course) of the Snowdon range, the coastline and the Rhinogs. Beneath one is a mountain riddled with mines which have been used for the storage of explosives. A few years ago there was a scare about whether the explosives had deteriorated to an extent that there was a danger to Llyn Stwlan's dam, and the lake was promptly emptied.

This is one of the wildest and most desolate sections of the Cambrian Way and can be very inhospitable in rain and cloudy conditions. Good map reading is particularly important here. From Moelwyn Mawr summit descent is made to the gaunt ruins of the Rhosydd quarry buildings. The peace of this area is likely to be shattered if permission is finally granted to open up quarries on the east side of the pass, despite much opposition. From the ruin buildings a faint path winds its way past small lakes to a point near Llyn yr Adar, where a left turn is made to join Poucher's route to the summit of Cnicht. ("The Welsh Peaks".)- Check Point 31.

At this point hostellers can retrace their steps to Llyn yr Adar and follow the path down to a minor road and thence by footpath, partly through forest, to Bryn Gwynant Youth Hostel. The latter part of this route (see map 45) leaves the public footpath shortly after leaving the forest, just beyond an old stone barn (marked on OS maps), and follows a permissive route for hostellers negotiated by the YHA with the landowner. The route is waymarked with white arrows and crosses into the extensive woods of the hostel grounds and so down steep paths to the hostel.

The main route continues down the south-west ridge of Cnicht, shown on OS1:50,000 map as a black dashed line. Some scrambling down is needed at a steep section not far belowthe summit where the best route is to the left (SE) side of the ridge. The gradient eases off and the route continues as a courtesy path waymarked by the national park, and is slightly different to Poucher's earlier editions in that it comes off the mountain at the pass on the Croesor to Nantmor track and not at

Croesor village itself. A look back to Cnicht shows it as quite an imposing mountain, but it is really an insult to the most famous mountain in the Alps to call it the "Welsh Matterhorn".

Due to an inconsistency between the definitive maps of the old Merioneth and Caernarfon counties, the old road crossing the former county boundary at 623452 is shown in different ways but it is a public highway down to Bwlchwernog A minor road is followed to Nantmor and a footpath to Pont Aberglaslyn. The old railway tunnel, now part of a circular walk from the national park car park at Nantmor, may be tempting, but nothing should deter our Connoisseur from viewing the spectacular cascade at Aberglaslyn Pass, as seen from the road bridge and more particularly from the exciting path alongside the river. The river path ascends to the old railway track, just beyond the north end of the tunnel. Fresh plans to reopen the Welsh Highland Railway may affect the fine walk along the old track. Where the railway crossed the river the old bridge can be used to cross sides of the river to visit the grave of Gelert, the faithful dog of Llewelyn the Great (see Richard Sale's book), but the more pleasant route is to keep on the east side into Beddgelert, and maybe pay homage to Gelert after refreshment .

Beddgelert to Pen-y-Pass via Snowdon
10 miles   3590 feet of ascent   Maps 44 & 45

Beddgelert is a deservedly popular tourist village, its main disadvantage being the traffic that pours through it and which in particular goes over the attractive bridge in the village centre. There are inns, shops, cafes and accommodation here. Considering that Beddgelert is only the same distance away from Snowdon summit as Llanberis, it has done little to develop a direct walking route to the country's highest mountain To get to the so-called " Beddgelert Path" would involve a ghastly 2 mile walk along the busy A4085 Caernarfon road. The original plans for Cambrian Way suggested the direct route via the ridge of Yr Aran, but the need to use rights of way wherever possible has led to a realisation that the Nant Gwynant approach alongside Llyn Dinas is so attractive that it is perhaps preferable anyway.

Hostellers from Bryn Gwynant come along the main road to join the main route at Pont Bethania, near the national park car park.

The Watkin Path is in many ways the most attractive approach to Snowdon, albeit the one involving the greatest ascent. The lower parts are on the track going to the old mines and quarries in Cwm Llan, and this has been skilfully restored in recent years by expert boulder movers as part of the Snowdon Management Scheme funded by the Countryside Commission .

The Watkin Path was opened by Gladstone in 1892, at the age of 84, during his fourth term of office as prime minister, the occasion being commemorated by a plaque on the Gladstone Rock. Supposedly Sir Edward Watkin had the path above the quarries made to the summit by a route to take in the view of the Snowdon Horseshoe but no account was taken of the impracticability of maintaining a good path across the very unstable south flank of Snowdon summit. Although large sums of money have been spent on Snowdon's paths, the upper part of the Watkin Path remains an unsolved and most intractable erosion problem. Fortunately however for Cambrian Way, there is no need to go that way at all as there is a better way up Allt Maenderyn and Bwlch Main ridge.

Just after passing some waterfalls and before the ruin of the mine manager's house, at 621520, an unsigned public footpath goes sharply left up an old incline.After 300 metres turn right onto the line of an old tramway and follow this for about another 300 metres, then strike half left towards the pass of Bwlch Cwm Llan.The line of the right of way is only vaguely discernible and peters out altogether nearer the pass. Once on Allt Maenderyn the way is up a broad rocky ridge. Some sections are getting eroded, mostly by those dashing down this ridge, but our Connoisseur, being on the ascent will add little to the erosion. The ridge is broad enough for the eroded parts to be bypassed but do not just walk on the edge of the

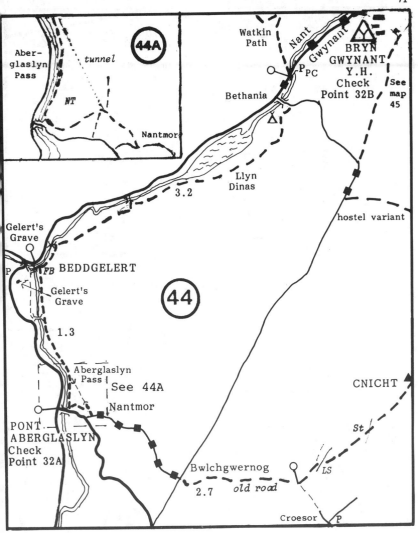

erosion - that's the next bit to go . Walk well away from the worn route - if all use was spread out the grass cover would not be damaged. Higher up the ridge narrows, particularly after being joined by the Llechog ridge and the route is slightly airy before the final scramble to the summit.

Snowdon summit will, more likely than not, be in cloud, even if the rest of the way up has been clear. Chris Jesty in his admirable panorama guide to Snowdon summit, reckons that the odds against seeing the nearby peak of Lliwedd as 1.1 to 1, with 400 to 1 against seeing Scafell Pike, the highest point in England.

The summit receives about 200 inches of rain and many hundreds of thousands of visitors a year. If you have ideas of celebrating reaching the climax of the Cambrian Way by sitting admiring the view with a pint of beer, at a table on a terrace at the cafe, then dispel this idea quickly. There may be so many in the cafe

Idwal Cottage

Llyn Ogwen

Gwern-y-gof Uchaf

Gwern-y-gof Isaf

PC

OGWEN

P

Heather Terrace

1.2

TRYFAN
3010' 917m

Llyn Idwal

Idwal Slabs

Llyn Bochlwyd

Bwlch Tryfan Bristly Ridge

0.5

Devil's Kitchen

Y Gribin

NT

Bwlch Caseg Fraith

GLYDER FAWR
3279' 999m
Check Point 34

1.7

GLYDER FACH
3262' 994m
Check Point 35

(46)

Miners' Track

1.5

Pen-y-gwryd Hotel

Pen-y-pass

Pen-y-gwryd Hotel

Pen-y-pass

PC P

Pen-y-pass

Grib Goch

Bwlch y Moch

Large Monolith

Pyg Track

Miners' Track

3.1

SNOWDON
3560' 1085m
Check Point 33

Llyn Llydau

Bwlch Main

Watkin Path

Lliwedd

(45)

Allt Maenderyn

Gladstone Rock

ruin

Llyn Gwynant

Und

3.7

ind

Tr

pa

waterfalls

Bryn Gwynant

Bwlch Cwm Llan

line of old tramways

Yr Aran

1.0

P PC

Bethania

Hostellers only route
hostel variant

that you refuse to wait to be served, there are no terraces with tables, and the cafe may be closed. It is only open when the railway is running, and does not open until some time after Easter because of snow in the railway cuttings. You are in a "dry" county of Wales and will not be served with beer on Sundays. Even a glass of water may be a problem as it all has to be brought up in the train.

Any soil that there once was near the summit pyramid has gone and serious suggestions have been made for people to be asked to carry small bags of earth up with them. The surroundings of the cafe and station are such that Prince Charles is said to have remarked that this is the highest slum in Britain. There have been plans for improvements but the costs of working at such a site are enormous.

Despite all the problems besetting Snowdon summit these do not alter the importance of Snowdon as the worthy climax of the Cambrian Way. It is a mountain on the grander scale than anything else en route and its magnificence is not belittled by its popularity.

From the summit area follow the path parallel to the railway to the enormous stone monolith at Bwlch Glas (spot height 993m) put up to indicate the vital point at which to hit the top of the Pyg or Pig Track. There is uncertainty as to whether the name of this famous path is derived from an abbreviation of the Pen-y-gwyrd Hotel beyond the end of the path or from the Welsh word "moch", sometimes meaning pig, in the title of the pass called Bwlch Moch part way up the path. At the monolith a decision must be made whether to follow the Pyg Track down or whether to take the more exciting but very exposed Crib Goch ridge route to Bwlch Moch. This classic part of the Snowdon Horseshoe route is strongly advised against if carrying a heavy pack, or if the walker is not very sure footed or if there are bad weather conditions. The ridge is really very knife-edged and quite sheer for hundreds of feet either side.

The Pyg Track has carried many millions intent on reaching the highest point in England and Wales under their own steam. It is only in recent years that it has been fully appreciated that such usage on such terrain requires maintenance to prevent the path becoming most unpleasant and dangerous to walk. This path is where most effort has been expended but the cost has been considerably reduced by the use of volunteers from several organisations notably the British Trust for Conservation Volunteers. If the idea of such public spirited work appeals to you, not necessarily on such arduous projects, contact B.T.C.V. at 35 St. Mary's Street, Wallingford, Oxon. for details of their national and local tasks.

The first section below the pass is appropriately called the Zig Zags and has been much improved. Do not be tempted to short cut as this is what caused such terrible erosion in the past. Further on there is another option, this time to descend to the Miners Track that runs up to the old mines by Llyn Glaslyn. This follows a wider path, crosses Llyn Llydaw by a causeway, and a much improved track to Peny-Pass. The Pyg track keeps higher up and crosses into the Llanberis valley at Bwlch Moch at the end of the Crib Goch ridge.

Pen-y-Pass, popular because at 1168 feet (356m) it is the highest road pass from which to climb Snowdon, consists of a youth hostel, restaurant and car park. Much to the disgust of many of the climbing fraternity the old Gorphwysfa Hotel at the pass was converted and extended, with large government grants, to become a very well appointed Youth Hostel. On the opposite side of the road is a cafe and toilets. If your mode of walking Cambrian Way involves the use of the car park, note that it is expensive and strictly limited in size. Hostel visitors have free overnight parking. There is nowhere else to park legally near the pass. The Snowdon Sherpa bus service calls here. A timetable is available from Snowdonia National Park Office; (see page 95). It is possible to use the buses so as to spend the night at say Peny Gwyrd, Llanberis, Beddgelert or Bryn Gwynant and return to resume the walk at Pen-y-Pass next day, thus allowing a light rucksack for Snowdon.

74

Pen-y-Pass to Ogwen via the Glyders
4.8 miles   2353 feet of ascent   Map 46

The path leading onto the Glyders is over a ladder stile on the Llanberis side of the hostel building. You then enter land owned by Mrs. Esme Kirby, of Dyffryn Mymbyr, near Capel Curig. She has been sheep farming this side of the Glyder range since the 1930s, when her former husband Thomas Firbank wrote the best selling book "I Bought a Mountain". The book is well worth reading, particularly for its insight into the problems of sheep farming in the wilder parts of Wales. Esme founded and was the driving force of the Snowdonia National Park Society.

The way up the broad south ridge of Glyder Fawr gets more defined as the years pass and is now marked as black dashes on the Landranger map. Compass and map work will be necessary in cloud in this area.. Assuming that the Ogwen valley is to be a staging point before the long trek over the Carneddau, our Connoisseur is advised either to have a short day from Pen-y-Pass to Ogwen or to get to Ogwen early enough to make separate sorties in this superb mountain area to, say, Tryfan or Cwm Idwal. By making Glyder Fach a checkpoint as well as Glyder Fawr use will be discouraged of the eroded descent from Glyder Fawr to Llyn Cwm and the frustrating boulder descent below the Devil's Kitchen. From Glyder Fach there are several possible descents, such as the Gribin or the very airy Bristly Ridge, but the recommended safe way is to proceed further east along the Glyder plateau to Bwlch Caseg Fraith, where the Miner's Track from Pen-y-Gwryd to Ogwen crosses over .

Tryfan, as the rockiest mountain in Wales is ideal for learning to climb (and the author has happy memories of the easier climbs there), but the north ridge is not for the uninitiated to descend with a large rucksack and therefore Tryfan has not been made a Cambrian Way checkpoint. The traverse of Tryfan is however a splendid expedition, but best achieved from north to south. On the top (3010 ft.) there are two prominent boulders, Adam and Eve. A mountaineer's initiation is sometimes to jump from one to the other.

From Bwlch Tryfan the Miner's Track passes Llyn Bochlwyd, an attractive spot, or a rougher way down is by Heather Terrace on the east side of Tryfan.

Ogwen has probably the finest panorama of mountains around it of anywhere in Wales and maybe this was why it gave its name to a rural district of Caernarvonshire before local government reorganisation in 1974. Certainly it was not the population living at Ogwen which gave it importance, since the place consists only of a mountain school, a Youth Hostel, tea bar, toilets and small car park. There is no pub or B&B . The National Trust owns virtually all the land you can see and does not allow camping except at the organised sites which are at Gwern Gof Isaf and Uchaf. This sounds a rather inhospitable place but it could be easily spoiled. Nearby at Cwm Idwal is a national nature reserve, and a pleasant evening stroll can be made from the hostel to follow the nature trail round Llyn Idwal, amidst the spellbinding scenery of the glacially carved valley.

Ogwen to Conwy via the Carneddau
18 miles   4697 feet of ascent   Maps 47 - 49

The final section of the Cambrian Way is longer than most other stages suggested but is not as long as the 28 mile final stretch of the Pennine Way. The journey can more easily be broken as there is a Youth Hostel about two-thirds of the way along, and a roadhead for car assisted parties near the Bwlch y Ddeufaen. On the other hand, this section has other hazards which can have serious consequences since 4½ miles run at over 3000 feet.At that level the mountains are more often in cloud than not, and just as much so in summer as winter. Conditions of rain, wind or snow can be unbelievably treacherous, as the author found with wind that just knocked one over and necessitated a retreat.There are escape routes but these can leave the walker in remote valleys miles from anywhere. There seems to be no satisfactory low level alternative route. If bad weather prevails on the last day of a

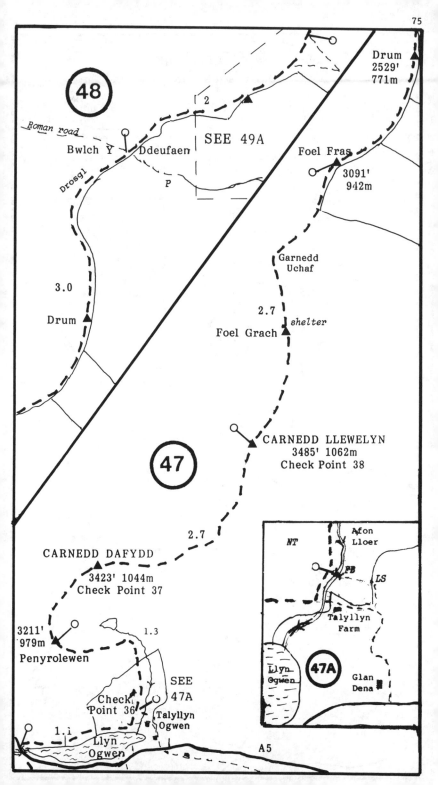

48

Roman road

Bwlch Y Ddeufaen

Drosgl

SEE 49A

P

2

3.0

Drum

Drum
2529'
771m

Foel Fras
3091'
942m

Garnedd
Uchaf

2.7

Foel Grach   *shelter*

CARNEDD LLEWELYN
3485' 1062m
Check Point 38

47

2.7

CARNEDD DAFYDD
3423' 1044m
Check Point 37

3211'
979m
Penyrolewen

1.3

Check
Point 36

SEE
47A

Talyllyn
Ogwen

1.1

Llyn
Ogwen

A5

NT

Afon
Lloer

FB

LS

Talyllyn
Farm

Llyn
Ogwen

47A

Glan
Dena

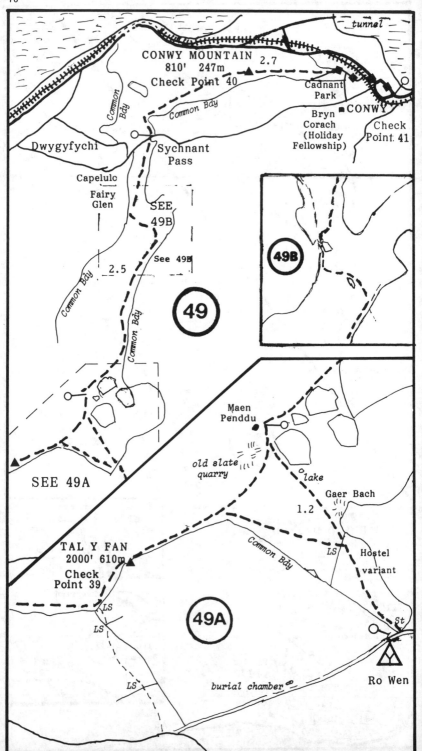

holiday and time does not permit an extra day discretion may be the better part of valour. On the other hand, navigation is not as difficult over the Carneddau as many parts of the Cambrian Way which may have already been traversed in cloud.

The whole way from Ogwen to Conwy is either National Trust land with unrestricted access (Ogwen to beyond Drum) or is over common land in former urban districts, some of it also crown common, and therefore with public right of access for air and exercise. Once over the stiles at Ogwen there are no more stiles or gates to negotiate on the main route.

Just over the road bridge at Ogwen go over the slate stile in the wall. This was put up in memory of Alfred Embleton, a Youth Hostel pioneer and for many years hon. treasurer of the Ramblers Association. The obvious route onto the Carneddau is straight up Penyrole-wen, average gradient 1 in 2½, but it has become frightfully eroded, unpleasant and dangerous, and is not recommended. Instead a longer and more pleasant way starts along the north side of Llyn Ogwen. The public footpath becomes undefined near Tal-y-llyn Ogwen Farm. Turn left before the river at the farm and proceed up, parallel to the river. Those who have stayed the night east of Llyn Ogwen can join the route here by the public footpath and permissive diversion at Talyllyn Ogwen Farm, (see map 47A). In order to discourage use of the eroded direct approach to Penyrole-wen the bridge north of the farm is a checkpoint. Note that the crossing of the Afon Lloer shown on the black dashed line on the Landranger map is not recommended . Head for a ladder stile and then when due east of the prominent crags on the left make for an obvious gully where an easy scramble leads up to the east ridge of Penyrole-wen. This can be difficult to find in cloud.

Most of the way along the Carneddau is on reasonably firm ground -no floundering in bog to get to a summit such as the Cheviot. Along the main ridge the way is usually visible on the ground though at places like north-west of Craig Llugwy the rocky ground does not reveal any path, and the drop on the left needs to be kept in view. The ridge is mostly broad north of Carnedd Llewelyn and it is easy to get off course. A sharp turn at Garnedd Uchaf for no apparent reason on open plateau needs to be watched for. Once a fence looms up on the right about half a mile before Foel Fras navigational worries should be over for the next five miles as one follows the west side of the fence all the way to beyond Tal-y-fan.

If making a detour to the delightful small hostel at Rowen, there are three options as to where to turn off the main route but one should bear in mind that- Tal-y-fan is a check point. The hostel variant leads down to a stile onto the steep road,then up 150metres to the hostel.

From Tal-y-fan (just 2000 feet) the way is across open common, mostly on rights of way, but the most spectacular section is a nondefinitive traverse path on an ex urban district common leading to Sychnant Pass. The road crossing was once the main coast road before tunnels were made in the cliff at Penmaen-bach Point.Those tunnels have been replaced with wider tunnels and since 1991 the Conwy estuary itself has been tunnelled under to preserve Conwy's character as a fine walled town which forms such a fitting climax to our walk.

Positively the last climb is over Conwy Mountain, a fine vantage point overlooking the sea and the north Wales coastline, as well as back to the Carneddau. Gorse and heather in late summer make this much path covered hill a most pleasant spot.

The castle at Conwy makes a fitting terminus for our long walk. The author hopes you have enjoyed it - you certainly won't forget it and his guess is that you will return to explore more of Wales you didn't know. You will find, as the author has done that the Welsh mountains grow on you. You will also wonder what all the fuss was about in the opposition to the Cambrian Way.

Comments about the walk, navigational problems, where you stayed or camped, and any comments about the book will be gratefully received by the author.

STAGE PLANNING

This section seeks to assist in planning to walk the Cambrian Way. It will be noted that heights of ascent are given against all distances. This must be taken very seriously into account in estimating the time required for each daily section.

Naismith's formula of three miles per hour plus half an hour per thousand feet is reduced to about two and a half miles an hour plus three quarters of an hour per thousand feet for those carrying heavy, packs . Slower walkers and leaders of parties (where inevitably the pace is that of the slowest), would be wiser to work on two miles per hour or less plus at least an hour per thousand feet.

Plan to finish well before sunset to allow for mistakes in navigation, fatigue and accidents, but as a precaution ensure that every member of a party has a torch that works, if only to read a map by when it is still possible to see one's way.

Distances in the chart below are derived from map measurements and are shown in miles, together with the feet of ascent, on lines in between the place name lines. The Y.H.A. and other variant columns show relevant distances and heights between dashes level with the places concerned.."Other variants" and their measurements are shown in italics.

The stages shown are not necessarily all suggested as daily sections and in some cases two or more sections may be covered in a day. More detailed distances are shown between flagged points on the 1:50,000 maps in this guide.

Cambrian Way is planned as a northbound excursion working up to a climax in Snowdonia. Do not be tempted to omit the Cardiff to Abergavenny section and then regret later on that the whole path has not been walked. It is well worth walking

STAGE PLANNER - SOUTHERN SECTION

Main Route Cumul Miles	Stage Miles Main Route	Feet of Ascent North-bound	Staging Points — Main Route	Staging Points — Variants	YHA Variants Miles	YHA Variants Asc.	Other Variants Miles	Other Variants Asc.
0			Cardiff Castle					
	5.4	125						
5.4			Tongwynlais					
	8.3	875						
13.7			Machen					
	3	1022						
16.7			Risca					
	8.2	1504						
24.9			Pontypool					
	11.3	1691						
36.2			Abergavenny		-		*10.7*	*2885*
	13.1	3443		*Llanthony*				
49.3			Capel y ffin	Capel y f.YH	14.2	3913	*11.6*	*2144*
	16.0	2652		*Pengenfordd*	15.5	2347	*10.2*	*2338*
65.3			Crickhowell		-		*13.9*	*1808*
	20.0	4896		Aber (Talybont)	21.7	2945	*10.7*	*3865*
85.3			Storey Arms					
				Llwyn y c.YH	-			
					7.3	1150	*12.1*	*1470*
	8.1	2183		Ystadfellte YH	-			
				Glyntawe	16.0	3000	-	
93.4			A4067 Bwlch Bryn-rhudd		17.3	4000		
	7.2	1940		Llanddeusant YH	-	-	*7*	*2040*
100.6			Llanddeusant/Trecastle rd.		-			
104.4	3.8	359	Myddfai		17.3	2500		
107.9	3.5	473	Llandovery	Bryn Poeth YH	-			
107.9	**21163**		Southern Section Sub Totals					

but do not try to "knock it off" in two days unless you are already very fit and are sure you can do it. Most people try to do too much in the early days of a long distance walk. After all, there's always Richard Sale's book on Cambrian Way to read in the evenings.

STAGE PLANNER - CENTRAL SECTION

Main Route Cumul Miles	Stage Miles Main Route	Feet of Ascent North-bound	Staging Points Main Route	Variants	YHA Variants Miles	Asc.	Other Variants Miles	Asc.
107.5			Llandovery		- 7.5	1483		
114.1	6.6	1033	Rhandirmwyn	Bryn Poeth YH	9.9	984		
126.1	12.0	1579	Nant y maen junc.	Tyncornel YH	- 7.4	950		
	6.6	946		Blaencaron YH	-		6.8	926
				Pontrhydfendigaid	-			
132.7			Strata Florida					
141.8	9.1	1408	Cwmystwyth		24.1	3944	10.5	1438
146.8	5.0	590	Devil's Bridge		-			
153.2	6.4	1340	Dyffryn Castell	Ystumtuen YH	-			
164.6	11.4	2560	Dylife					
173.2	8.6	750	Commins Coch					
186.2	13.0	2460	Dinas Mawddwy					
78.7		**12666**	**Central Section Sub Totals**					

STAGE PLANNER - NORTHERN (SNOWDONIA) SECTION

Main Route Cumul Miles	Stage Miles Main Route	Feet of Ascent North-bound	Staging Points Main Route	Variants	YHA Variants Miles	Asc.	Other Variants Miles	Asc.
186.2	8.6	2883	Dinas Mawddwy		-		- 10.8	2883
194.8			Bwlch Llyn Bach A487		15.0	5096		
	11.3	2643		Minffordd	-		- 11.0	3048
				Kings YH	- 5.6	700		
206.1			Barmouth		-		- 13.4	3882
	13.8	5534		Cwm Nantcol Tel.	16.7	4118	-	
				Llanbedr YH	- 4.4	580		
			Cwm Na.(Maes y garnedd)		-		-	
219.9	8.5	2394	Cwm Bychan		15.5	4740	12.6	4230
228.4			Maentwrog		-		-	
241.2	12.8	3617	Beddgelert	Ffestiniog YH	- 10.2	3347		
	10.0	3590		Bryn Gwynant YH	- 7.8	3360		
251.2	4.8	2353	Pen y Pass	YH	- 4.8	2353		
256.0			Ogwen	Idwal Cott.YH	13.5	4388		
	18.3	4697		Rowen YH	- 6.4	9-09		
274.3			Conwy Castle		-			
88.1		**27711**	**Northern Section Sub Totals**					

274.3		**61540**	**GRAND TOTAL CAMBRIAN WAY**					

MAPS FOR CAMBRIAN WAY

Maps are **absolutely essential** for navigation on the Cambrian Way., Much of the way is undefined on the ground and those used to the Pennine Way and most other long distance paths will find they have to be good map readers and that time must be allowed for frequent looks at the maps .

The maps in this guidebook are designed to be read in conjunction with the Ordnance Survey 1: 50,000 Landranger maps and **are not intended to be used on their own**.

Map reading ability is essential to avoid unnecessary trespass and aggravation of farmers. Just a few bad map readers can incur the quite justifiable wrath of farmers if they climb over walls and fences where they have no right to go.

General Map. For planning purposes, sorting out one's travel to and from the area, and worth taking for identifying distant views is the Ordnance Survey's 1:250,000 Travelmaster map, sheet 7, Wales and West Midlands, price £3.99 (1995). This map shows the mountain ranges clearly and marks railways and youth hostels.

1:50,000 (about 1¼ inch to the mile) **Landranger Series**. 7 maps are required at £4.50 (1995). These maps show public rights of way but not field boundaries. The maps on pages 16 and 17 give the key to these maps as well as to the strip maps in this guide. Note that there is an option between maps 146 and 147. Map 147 (Elan Valley and Builth Wells) is the map for walking the Elenydd - the wildest part of Wales, but it just omits Tregaron and part of its Bog, which come on map 146. The weight of seven maps is 1lb (700 grams) but this can be reduced by removing the covers and cutting to about half or a third of the area. The flat,unfolded versions are the same price but usually have to be ordered from shops.

1:25,000 (about 2½ inches to the mile). This scale is very desirable but not essential for following the Cambrian Way as the inset maps in this guide show enough detail to facilitate navigation in the valley sections, where field boundary information is important. If however, weight and cost considerations are not important, maps at this scale can enhance the enjoyment of the walk and ease navigation . The O.S . **Leisure Map** series at this scale covers the Snowdonia National Park sections of Cambrian Way on three double sided maps. Cambrian Way traverses all three single sided Leisure Maps of the Brecon Beacons National Park. The rest of the route is covered by the **Pathfinder** series, of which 15 are required for complete coverage, together with the Leisure Maps just mentioned. Costs (1995) - Leisure maps £5.25, Pathfinder £3.95. The cost of the maps at this scale would be £90.75 and the weight 3lbs. (1362 grams) . Undoubtedly the best value are the three Snowdonia maps but note the advice about when to turn the Cadair map over on page 61.

The Maps in this guide are of three kinds:-

1. **Key maps** - (a) South and (b) North, showing layout of the 1:50,000 strip maps and to the 1: 50,000 Ordnance Survey Landranger maps . See pages 16 and 17.

2 . **1: 50,000 strip maps** covering the whole route, derived from out of copyright one inch to mile (1:63,360) Ordnance Survey maps of the 1920s, together with observed additions or amendments, and enlarged to 1: 50,000 for convenience of readers' comparison with the current O.S. maps of that scale. They are serial numbered from the south end. North is at the top of each map unless otherwise marked.

3. **Inset maps** covering parts of the route, usually at 1:25,000 scale but some at six inch to mile (1:10,560) or other scales. These are derived from out of copyright six inch to the mile Ordnance Survey maps of about 1905 . The scale has been contracted to 1:25,000 as being a scale familiar to walkers and one at which one can conveniently show field boundaries . Again all maps have north at the top unless otherwise marked.The maps are numbered with a letter following the number of the 1:50,000 map of which they are an enlargement.Thus 25B is the second inset map to map 25.

Map Carrying Particular attention needs to be paid to the problems of frequently referring to both the O.S.1:50,000 maps and to the maps in this guide book. Misnavigation is usually due to not looking at the maps often enough and this in turn is usually due to the physical difficulties of viewing them easily. It may be easy enough to refer to them if the weather is fine and the user has large cagoule pockets, but what if it is raining or blowing a gale? If it is too hot to wear a cagoule or jacket will the maps go in the pockets of one's lower garment?

Ideally one needs an arrangement whereby the two maps and the description can be viewed through the transparent plastic of a bag that can be folded up and the whole affair slipped into a hip pocket when not in use. This ideal is well nigh impossible without some compromise.

Map cases are usually about ten inches square and will take an O.S. map bent over ,as it is not meant to be, to show two segments each side. Most map cases are too rigid to go in a pocket and have a cord so that they can be suspended round the neck. The author of this guide is one who detests such flapping cases and often uses a 15"x 20" "Seal again" plastic bag which will take an O.S. map with four segments showing one way, and without distorting the map from its normal folds. The bag is pliable enough to fold with the map and go in a pocket. *Whatever arrangement the reader comes to must make it easy to refer to both 1:50,000 OS map and the guidebook strip map at any time.*

A compromise that can be made is to reduce the bulk of both the O.S. map and the guide book. For a start the covers of the maps can be removed (or buy flat maps) and the maps cut in size. As regards this guide book, it has been arranged that the pages of route description and maps are in the centre of the book so that they can be removed by opening the staples. Thus only the map and description in use need be in the map carrier.

Pockets for maps can also be a problem. Walking and climbing breeches usually have good deep pockets with zip or button fastening but jeans and shorts usually have uselessly small pockets.

WEATHER FORECASTS

Commercial weather services at 39p per minute evenings and weekends 49p per minute peak and standard times . There are several alternative services, varying in length, quality and in frequency of update.

"Weathercall" 0891 500 then 409 for Gwent & Glamorgan (S.Wales), 414 Dyfed & Powys (Central Wales), 415 Gwynedd & Clwyd (North Wales). 5 Day forecasts 0891 5053 (24 hour forecast by FAX 4499) +09 Glamorgan & Gwent, 14 Dyfed & Powys, 15 Gwynedd & Clwyd.

"Mountaincall" for Snowdonia, 0891 500 449 gives cloud heights, and mountain conditions, followed by longer term forecast for Wales.

Ramblers "Weatherline" 0891 1684 +38 South Wales and 39 North Wales - short and chatty (less than one minute) but not so comprehensive. Useful if you haven't much change at a phone box. (30% of revenue goes to the Rambler Association)

METRIC/IMPERIAL CONVERSION SLIDE RULE

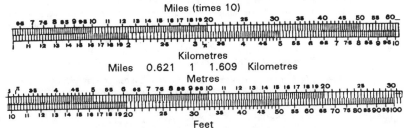

Miles (times 10)

Kilometres

Miles   0.621   1   1.609   Kilometres

Metres

Feet

Feet 3.281 1 0.305 metres

YOUTH HOSTEL SECTION

The Cambrian Way is blessed with a chain of Youth Hostels which is already more complete than was available on the Pennine Way when that Path was opened. Those who desire a roof over their heads at night will find it is almost essential to use hostels in some of the central Wales sections, and even in the heart of Snowdonia, there is only Youth Hostel accommodation at Pen-y-pass and Ogwen. At between half and three quarters of the price of bed and breakfast establishments they provide at least basic needs and in some cases almost luxurious facilities, together with a friendly atmosphere and understanding of walkers' needs. The facility to make a meal quite late at night, and early in the morning gives hostellers much greater flexibility than staying in commercial accommodation. Whilst the higher grade and larger hostels have greater facilities and comfort, some veteran hostellers may find the exuberance of large parties of youngsters somewhat wearing. They may find the smaller simpler hostels in south and central Wales more to their liking. The simple hostels of South Wales are renowned for being "what hostelling is all about", and this had recognition when the group of four hostels in the Elenyth (Bryn Poeth, Dolgoch, Tyncornel and Blaencaron) received priority treatment during 1988 and 1989.

Membership of YHA is necessary. 1995 fees are senior £9.00, Under 18 £3.00. (including accommodation guide which from 1995 will be sent by post to members) Membership fees can be paid at any hostel, or at YHA shops such as Cardiff, or to Head Office..

Overnight fees vary according to the scale rate for the hostel. 1995 fees on the Cambrian Way hostels vary from £5.35 at the simple, scale 1, hostels up to £8.80 for scale 6 hostels at Cardiff and Pen-y-pass . Under 18 members pay about two-thirds of senior rate. Booking in advance is normally direct to the warden but at the time of writing is to the Regional Office at Cardiff for Tyncornel, and Dolgoch, and through Colwyn Bay Hostel for Rowen. There is a booking bureaux for Ystradfellte, Llanddeusant, Bryn Poeth Uchaf, Tyncornel, Dolgoch, Blaencaron and Ystumtuen through the Wales Regional Office. at Cardiff. Details are given in the YHA Accommodation Guide on the Mid Wales introductory page. Telephone bookings cannot be guaranteed without payment, and should only be made during hostel opening hours (before 1000 and after 1700) and preferably not during meal times. Firm bookings by telephone can be made using Access or Visa cards, except at Bryn Poeth Uchaf, Tyncornel, and Corris. All hostels can be full in holiday periods but meals provided hostels can also get booked up in May, June and early July with school parties. Be particularly watchful of weekly closing nights for warden's day off. Some hostels have a self-cooking night and other hostels are open all the week. Very few small hostels are open in the winter months, though some, may be willing to open for parties of walkers.

At the hostels where meals are provided, these should be booked and paid for in advance. The evening meal can also be booked if arrival is made before 6 p.m.. The evening meal is at a set time, usually 7 pm . 1995 prices are from £4 for evening meal and £2.70 for breakfast. A standard packed lunch costs £2.20. All hostels have a members kitchen where all utensils are provided for preparing, cooking and eating meals. Most have refrigerators and a few have microwave ovens. Most hostels have stores of basic food to sell but at the remoter hostels too much reliance should not be placed on them - see notes under individual hostels. Fresh milk and bread should be ordered in advance but are often available on arrival.

Sleeping is in dormitories of varying sizes. Sexes are segregated, but at some hostels there are small rooms which the wardens can allow for family use. All hostellers must use a sheet sleeping bag. but these are now provided as part of the bednight fee so there is no need to carry one..

Camping is allowed at eight of the hostels listed below at half the senior bednight fee regardless of age. Campers can use the hostel facilities but must not take hostel bedding or utensils to their tents.

Booking into hostels can be up to 10.30p.m. Hostellers are expected to be in by 11 and lights out is usually at 11.30 p.m. Rising before 7.0 am is frowned on as it may disturb others who want to have a full nights sleep. Many long distance walkers will, however, find it frustrating to wait until 8.0 or even 8.30 for the hostel breakfast and prefer to get their own. Tell the warden if you want to make an early getaway. Times are generally more flexible at the smaller more remote hostels . Twenty hostels are listed below. Some are too close together to be used by all except very slow walkers but the average keen hosteller is likely to use about fourteen. Very regrettably five hostels have closed down in recent years and have not been replaced. These were Gerddi Bluog in the Rhinogau, Harlech, Penmaenmawr, Crickhowell, Dinas Mawddwy and Ffestiniog.

Y.H.A. OFFICES AND SHOP

Youth Hostels Association (England & Wales) , National Office, Trevelyan House, 8 St. Stephens Hill, St. Albans, Herts, AL1 2DY. ☎.01727 855215. For membership & accommodation guide.

Wales Regional Office , 4th Floor, 1 Cathedral Rd., Cardiff , CF1 9HA . ☎01222 396766 for hostel enquiries, bookings for Tyncornel and Dolgoch, and for Mid Wales booking bureau.

YHA Adventure Shop, 13 Castle St. (opposite the Castle), Cardiff, ☎01222 399178. Open Mon-Sat. 9.30 to 5.30. For enrolments and large selection of walking and camping equipment. *YHA members get 10% discount.*
Blacks Camping & Leisure is at 17 Castle St.

HOSTELS BY OR NEAR THE CAMBRIAN WAY (1995 information)
For full postal addresses see YHA Accommodation Guide

Cardiff at ST184789 , 2 Wedal Rd ., Roath Park, Cardiff, scale 6. ☎01222 462303, 68 beds. This hostel is very popular with the internationals, so booking can be important . EM 7pm plus cafeteria and snack service No closing night between March and October. Two miles from start of Cambrian Way (bus services). Open from 3 pm.

Llwyn-y-pia, (pronounced Thlooinapeea) Rhondda Valley, at SS993939 (1:50,000 map 170), 62 beds, scale 5. ☎01443 430859. Hostel ½ mile from station. Closed Saturdays and Sundays except bank holiday weekends. Glyncornel Environmental Studies Centre and hostel are in a former mineowner's house, more recently a hospital, in extensive wooded grounds above industrialised valley. Hostel is near the area immortalised in " How Green was my Valley" . There is a mining museum at the hostel. Although 14 miles from the Cambrian Way at Tongwynlais, trains run regularly to and from Radyr and Taffs Well.

Capel-y-ffin, Black Mountains, at SO250328, 40 beds plus limited camping, scale 3. ☎Crucorney 01873 890650 . Bread and milk must be ordered at least a week in advance. Closed every Wednesday, July/August no meals provided on Wednesdays but self catering available. Resident warden. Drying facilities, showers. This homely and magnificently situated hostel is in a former farmhouse converted from King George VI Memorial Fund. It is popular for pony trekking and Offa's Dyke path walkers, so booking is important.

Llwyn-y-celyn (pronounced "thlooinakellin"), Brecon Beacons, at SN973225, 46 beds, scale 3. ☎01874 624261. Generally closed Sundays except mid July to end of September. Like Capel-y-ffin, this hostel was once the highest farm in its valley. Attractive surroundings with scattered natural woodland around and nature reserve nearby.

Ystradfellte (pronounced "Ustradvethta"), south of Brecon Beacons at SN925127, 28 beds, simple, scale 2. ☎01639 720301. Closed Thursdays except mid-July to end of August. No meals provided. Shop open mornings near church and pub at 930134. Common room and one dormitory in house across the road. Very fine waterfall and cave country that is well worth a day's stopover .

Llanddeusant (pronounced "Thlandysant") at SN776245, 28 beds, simple, scale 2. ☎015504 634 or 619. No closing night. No meals provided. Hot shower. Central heating. Hostel was once the Old Red Lion Inn, though it is difficult to imagine how this tiny hamlet supported a pub. No hostel shop. No bread or milk. Nearest shop 1 ½ miles away. Stock up at Llwyn-y-celyn or Ystradfellte or even Crickhowell. .

Bryn Poeth Uchaf, A mile east of Rhandirmwyn, at SN796439, 22 beds, including a family unit, simple, scale 1. ☎(warden) 015505 235. No meals provided. No closing night. Book in at warden's farmhouse, Hafod-y-pant (SN800432), then follow waymarked path for three-quarters of a mile up to hostel, which is an old farmhouse, lit by gaslight and very isolated. Views back to Brecon Beacons. Most remote of the hostels as no vehicular access. Difficult to find after dark. Warden has no stores and does not sell bread or milk, so stock up in Llandovery. Drying facilities if you light the fire. Hot shower. Waymarked path on to Rhandirmwyn.

Tyncornel, at SN751534, 16 beds, simple, scale 1. No telephone. No meals provided. No closing night. Only way of booking in advance is by post to Regional Office. In some respects more remote than Bryn Poeth, although there is a long narrow road, (rough for the last mile), to the hostel from Llandewi Brefi. No hostel shop so stock up at the post office at Rhandirmwyn (next shops at Pontrhydfendigaid unless detour is made to Tregaron) . Hostel is former farmhouse. Gas lighting. Drying facilities if you light the fire. Hot shower. Wardens at this hostel are volunteers who come for a week at a time.

Dolgoch, at SN806561, 22 beds, simple, scale 1.☎01974 298680 . Bookings to Regional Office. No meals provided . No closing night. Volunteer warden. Gas lighting. Hot shower, small store. Although well off the route this old farmhouse can be rung up to ascertain availability of   beds during that week..

Blaencaron at SN713608, 16 beds, simple, scale 1. This hostel was once noted as being in a primitive class of its own and was in danger of being closed but the Countryside Commission came to the rescue and provided   a 50% grant which enabled the old school premises to have a complete internal rearrangement and the provision of flush toilets, showers, and drying facilities. No closing night. No meals provided. No hostel store. Warden lives ¾mile away at SN706609, ☎01974 298441.

Ystumtuen (pronounced "Ustumteean"), at SN735786, 24 beds, simple scale 1. ☎.(warden) 01970 890693. No meals provided . No closing night. This hostel is a former school next to a chapel in a quiet village in attractive hilly country that was once a scene of much lead mining, Toilets are up the garden path. Hot shower and drying room with fan heater. There is a very interesting mining museum and a cafe three miles away at Llywernog.(SN733809). The warden lives nearby and has a small store.

Corris at SH753080, 42 beds, simple, scale 1. ☎01654 761686. Privately run hostel providing meals. Small store at hostel and PO/shop in village (ECD Wed./Sat) . Another former school but with central heating. No closing night. A family room is sometimes available. Showers. Corris is a former slate quarrying village in spectacular wooded surroundings. It has a railway museum and a craft centre, and 3 miles to the south is the Centre for Alternative Technology. Divergence from the main route can be made at Mynydd Ceiswyn, thence via Cwm Ratgoed and Aberllefenni making 11.3 miles from Dinas Mawddwy. Corris to Cader Idris involves a minimum of 1.2 miles of the A487 and distances are 9.1 miles to Kings (plus 2933' of ascent) and 14 miles to Barmouth.

Kings, Dolgellau, at SH683161, 56 beds, camping, scale 3. ☎01341 422392. Showers. Closing nights Sunday or Sun.& Mon,except July & Aug. House in idyllic wooded valley setting with river running through grounds. Some dormitories in large refurbished outbuilding. Check on access into house and kitchen if leaving early in morning. Members' kitchen can get congested. Strategically awkwardly placed for next night's stop unless camping on the Rhinogs or diverging to Llanbedr. (or an easy day to Barmouth)

Llanbedr at SH585267, 48 beds, family room, scale 3. ☎01341 241287. Showers. Closing night Monday. May/June, except bank holiday weekends. Sun./Mon Sept/Oct. House by main road where it crosses river Artro.

Bryn Gwynant at SH641513, 70 beds, family room, camping, scale 5. ☎01766 890251. Showers. Good drying room. No closing night in summer but hostel closed first two weeks of September . Magnificently situated former mansion in 40 acres of grounds overlooking Llyn Gwynant. . Access from public footpath at SH643511 by courtesy path for hostellers only, waymarked by the author with white arrows.

Pen-y-pass at SH647556, 104 beds, family rooms, scale 6, limited daytime access. ☎01286 870428. No closing night Apr -Oct. Showers. Formerly a famous climbers' pub on the pass, converted and added to at great expense to become the largest hostel in Snowdonia. At least the pass is quieter in the evening after the hordes who walk up Snowdon from here have gone away.

Idwal Cottage, Ogwen, at SH648603, 56 beds, scale 3. ☎01248 600225. Showers. Closing night Sunday Apr-Jun, & Sept. Closed early Sept..Some dormitories in former chapel nearby. Mountain rescue post . Well situated at focal point of wild and popular mountain area. Booking important as no other accommodation at Ogwen.

Capel Curig at SH726579, 60 beds, scale 5, ☎016904 225, showers, Closing nights Sun & Mon in September. Useful if Idwal Cottage is full or closed. Sherpa bus service can be used for return to Ogwen in the morning.

Rowen, North Carneddau, at SH747721, 24 beds, simple, scale 1. ☎01492 531406. All bookings through Colwyn Bay Hostel (see below). Wardens are volunteers on weekly basis. No meals provided. Open at Easter and May to August No closing night Hurray for return to a small hostel. A gem set half way up side of Tal-y-Fan, in an old farmhouse. Enables the long trek across the Carneddau to be broken up leaving a half day on to the finish at Conwy. No stores, bread or milk. Shop is 1½ miles away and 700ft below .

Colwyn Bay, at SH847776, is the nearest hostel to the northern terminus of the Cambrian Way and accessible via train or bus to the coastal resort of Colwyn Bay and thence by minor road into country again for a mile to hostel which is a large country house in extensive grounds. 87 beds, scale 3, ☎01492 530627. Closing night Sun.Apr-Jun <u>&</u> Sun/Mon Sept-Oct.

ACCOMMODATION & SERVICES

This section includes principally bed and breakfast addresses, small hotels and camp sites, but also includes some inns providing meals, cafes, food shops, village post offices and a taxi service. Youth hostels are listed without full detail, as they are more comprehensively covered in pages 82 to 85.

No fee or inducement has been accepted for any entry. This list is provided purely as a service to Cambrian Way walkers. Entry is entirely at the discretion of the author. Almost all have been personally visited by the author and about half have actually been used for overnight accommodation.Whilst every effort has been made to secure accuracy of the information provided nevertheless the author accepts no responsibity for errors or for the standards of accommodation or other services provided.

Place names are given in capital letters followed by the postal address, and the telephone dialling code, e.g. LLANTHONY, Abergavenny, Gwent. ☎ 01873

Grid References are given thus:- SO123456. A full explanation of how to read a grid reference is on every Ordnance Survey Landranger and Pathfinder map.

Rooms - number of rooms in each category are given as D = double bed, T = twin beds, F = family rooms,(usually a double and one or more single beds) S = single bed. ES = en suite, i.e private toilet with bath or shower or both. Absence of ES does not mean such facilities are not available.

Prices are normally the basic bed and breakfast price per person. Note that single prices may be more and many establishments have several different prices. The figure in brackets after the price indicates the year for which prices were last checked by the author, e.g. ('95 = 1995). If this is a year or so before publication it does not necessarily mean that the author is unaware whether it is still in business but it makes prior booking more essential. In any case prices are liable to rise, not least because of improvements such as the provision of en suite facilities.

Meals - EM means evening meal provided, EMO to order only. It is always wise not to expect a meal if arriving without booking. The price if given is only a rough guide at the date obtained. SB = bar snacks in a pub,

Amendments to the list which follow will be made, as known, to the master list held by the author, and an amendment sheet issued attached to the inside back cover. For the latest list readers are advised to ring the author about availability of lists or send 50p and a stamped addressed envelope to the address on page 1.

The Cambrian Way Association is a consortium of five bed and breakfast operators who provide transport to and from the Cambrian Way to enable walkers to have the same base for several nights. An information pack and logbook can be obtained from the organiser, Nick Bointon, (see under Rhandirmwyn, page 89). The Association is not a membership organisation like the Offa's Dyke Association or South-West Way associations. **Guided walks** along Cambrian Way for strong walkers are provided by **High Trek,Snowdonia,** Tal y Waen,Deiniolen,Gwynedd LL55 3NA, ☎01286 871232 using Association hotels. Costs in 1995 were £450 for 1 week and £1200 for 3.

Stilwell's National Trail Companion Accommodation Guide 1996 is expected to have a section on Cambrian Way. Information is derived from computerised lists and information provided by the operators, and not from personal visits and on site ascertainment of grid references.

CARDIFF, South Glamorgan.   ☎01222
    Accommodation list from City Hall, Cardiff.
    Youth Hostel, ST184789, 68 beds, - see separate list.
    Bon Maison, 39 Plasturton Gardens,(parallel to Cathedral Rd.) CF1 9HG,
        ST170769, Mrs.M.A.George, ☎ .383660, T2 D2 F1 £15-£17.50 ('95), EMO,
        TMF, breakfast from 7.30.
    There are several hotels in Cathedral Rd area,around ST171770.
    Peppermill Restaurant,ST167770, EM except Sunday.

TONGWYNLAIS, Cardiff.
Three pubs and a fish and chip shop,ST133822.

LLWYNYPIA, Rhondda Valley, Mid Glamorgan. (by train from Radyr or Taffs Well)
Youth Hostel, Glyncornel Centre, SS993939, see separate list.

THORNHILL, Caerphilly, Mid Glamorgan.   ☎ 01222
Travellers Rest Inn, ST158843, ☎886894, SB, No accommodation.

RUDRY, Caerphilly, Mid Glamorgan.   ☎01222
    Maenllwyd Inn, ST201866, SB, No accommodation.
    Griffin Motel, CF8 3EA, ST193866, Mrs.E.L.Evans, ☎883396,
        32rooms (ES), £45S, £50D, Reduced weekend prices,('95), Restaurant.

MACHEN, Newport, Gwent.   ☎ 01633
    Brynteg, White Hart, ST204891, Mr.T.E.Jones, 440280, £13.50
    ('95), S1 D2 T1, EM at pub. 3min walk

NEWPORT, Gwent. (bus stop for Risca at Oakfield Rd, ST302879.)   ☎01633
    Caerleon House Hotel, Caerau Rd, ST304878, Judy Grundy & Jeff Shepherd,
        ☎264869, £17.50 - £22
    Arundel, 26 Chepstow Rd, NP9 8EA, ST318885, Mrs. Harrington, ☎267297,
        S2, D3, £13/14 ('95).

RISCA, Newport, Gwent.
    Westwood Villa Guest H'se, 59 Risca Rd, Crosskeys, NP1 7BT,
        ST223917, Bob & Maureen Evans, ☎ 01495 270336, S1 D3 F2 fr £15/22 (95)
    Darren Inn, ST234915 ☎01633 612414, SB.
    Ynys Hywel camping barn, at Countryside Centre, Cwmfelinfach
        Crosskeys, ST188913, Warden ☎01495 200113, sleeps 8,
        woodburning stove, no electricity, , £2.50
    Nant Carn Valley Camp Site, (Islwyn Borough Council), ST230935,
        toilets, wash basins, £1.70 per tent ('88).

PONTYPOOL, Gwent.   ☎ 01495
    Mountain Air Inn, ST277979, SB, .
    Lamb Inn, ST282991,SB.
    Lyndhurst, Park View, SO286004, NP4 5JT,Pam & Bill Stopgate, ☎764598, S2
        D1 F1 £12('95), No cooked breakfast.
    Pentwyn Farm, Little Mill, SO325035 ,NP4 OHQ , Mrs Ann Bradley, ☎228249,
        D1 T1 F1 £13/17 ('95). EMO. Transport to & from Pontypool.
    Ty'r Ywen, Mamhilad, SO296046, Mrs Susan Armitage, ☎.785200
        ,D3 T1 ES £19/20,£35 with Jacuzzi ('95), EM.
    Goose & Cuckoo Inn, SO291073, SB, ☎ 01873 880277.

ABERGAVENNY, Gwent   ☎01873
> Tourist Information & National Park Centre, Monmouth Rd, SO301140,
>   ☎857588, for accommodation lists and bookings.
> Halidon House, 63 Monmouth Rd, SO303137,Mrs Noni Heritage,
>   ☎857855, S1 D2 T1 ,£17.50 S£15 ('95)
> Belchamps Guest House, 1 Holywell Rd, NP7 5LP, SO302139, Ann & Arthur
>   Rogers, ☎853204, £18('95)
> Pysgodlyn Farm, SO261155, Camping. Mr.K.T.Davies, ☎853271.
> Smithy's Bunkhouse, Lower House Farm, Pantgelli, SO304178, Neil Smith,
>   ☎853432, sleeps 24 (2X12), self catering, SB at pub.

LLANTHONY, Abergavenny,Gwent.   ☎01873
> Half Moon Inn, SO286279, NP7 7NN, Christine Smith, ☎890611, D4 T2 F1
>   £17/20 F£14.50 ('95)
> Abbey Hotel, SO288278, NP7 7NN, ☎890487, D4,£41 ('92).
> Court Farm, SO288277, NP7 7NN, Camping,

CAPEL Y FFIN, Abergavenny.Gwent.   ☎01873
> Youth Hostel, SO250328, 38 beds, see separate list.
> Grange Pony Trekking Centre, SO251315, Mrs.Griffiths, NP7 7NP,
>   ☎890215, T2 F3, £20 ('95), EM £20, camping.
> Chapel Farm, SO254315, camping

PENGENFORDD, Talgarth,Powys   ☎01874
> Castle Inn, SO174296., Doug.& Beryl Webb, ☎711353, D2 £18('95), SB,
>   camping.
> Cwmfforest Guest Farm, SO182292, Mrs Turner, ☎711398, D3 EMO, Pony
>   Trekking Centre.

CRICKHOWELL, Powys.   ☎01873
> Dragon Hotel, High St., NP8 1BE, SO217183, Alan & Christine Thomas,
>   ☎810362, 17rooms (9ES),D3 T8 F3 S3, £19(23ES) ('93), Minibus
>   transport arranged to and from Cambrian Way for stages between
>   Cardiff and Brecon Beacons, See note page 86
> 2 Greenhill Villas,Beaufort St., NP8 1AL, SO220182, Ian & Lona Morgan,
>   ☎811177, D1 F2, £13/15 ('93)
> Carlton House,High St., SO217183, Mrs Linda Morgan, ☎810507,D1ES
>   £15('93).
> Riverside Caravan & Camping Park, New Rd, SO215184, ☎810397,

CWM CRAWNON   ☎01874
> Pyrgad, SO101159, Mr. Probert, ☎730558,Camping,basic, water,no facilities.

TALYBONT ON USK, / ABER, Brecon,Powys.   ☎01874
> Abercynafon Lodge, SO080175, Mrs J.Carr, LD3 7YT ☎676342, D1 T1 S1,
>   £13 EMO.
> Shop House, SO105214, Mrs.M.Taylor, Aber, LD3 7YS, ☎676276, T2 £12,(94)
> Yew Tree Cottage, SO105214 Aber Village, LD3 7YS, , Mr.& Mrs.Carroll,
>   ☎676276, T1 £15,('95) EMO,
> Brynhyfryd, Talybont, SO116224, Mrs.M.Evans, ☎676230, D1 T1 F2, £20
>   ('95), EMO for parties.
> Talybont ----3 pubs plus hotel with SB and B&B.
> Camp site (National Park), SO105209, basic,water,toilets.

STOREY ARMS / LIBANUS, Brecon,Powys.
Youth Hostel, Llwyn-y-celyn, SO973225, 46 beds, see separate list.

YSTRADFELLTE, Aberdare, Mid Glamorgan.   ☎01639
Youth Hostel, SO925127, 28 beds,see separate list.
Ty-y-Berllan, SN930134, Mrs.L.Barry, ☎722242, D3 £12.50 ('92),EMO.
Maes-y-ronnen, SO929135, Mrs Morgan,☎ 722343, D1 T1,£12-14('92)
Clyn-gwyn Farm, SN921107, Mrs Latham, ☎ 722255, F1 £15('92), EMO,
6 berth caravan £5 per person.
Village shop, SO930135, open mornings.

GLYNTAWE, Pen-y-cae, Abercrave, Swansea, West Glamorgan.   ☎01639
Dderi Farm, SN851174,SA9 1GT, Mrs.Jennifer Williams, ☎730458, F1 £16 ('93)
Dan-yr-Ogof Caves Motel, SN840161, SA9 1GF,,☎730284, £25 D room,£20S
ES,TMF, continental breakfast, also camping ground, SN843163
Gwyn Arms, SN846165 ☎730310, Restaurant
Tafarn-y-garreg Inn, SN849171, ☎ 730267 SB
Blaen Twyni Farm, camping, SN852173, Mrs.E.Benham, ☎730664

CRAI. Brecon, Powys.   ☎01874
Llwynhir Farm, SN893242, LD3 8YW, Mrs.A.Harris, ☎636563, D2 S1 £15
('95) EM (Light meal)

LLANDDEUSANT,Llangadog,Dyfed.
Youth Hostel, SN776245, 28 beds, see separate list.
Cross Inn, SN773258, SB, camping, caravans, shop.

MYDDFAI, Llandovery, Dyfed.   ☎01550
Plough Inn, SN772301,SA20 0NZ, ☎720643, D1 T1 S1 £15 ('95),SB
Erwlas, SN768307, SA20 0JB, Margaret & John Holloway, ☎720797, D1
T1 £12.50 ('93) EMO £5.

LLANDOVERY, Dyfed.   ☎01550
Llwyncelyn Guest House, Chainbridge, SN761347, SA20 0EP, , Mrs. Griffiths,
☎720566, D1 T3 F1 S1, £18('94), EM £11.50 (7pm).
Drovers Restaurant, 9 Market Square, SN767343, Jill & Michael Blud,
☎721115, D2 T1 £15-18 ('93)
King Head Inn,(16th cent), Market Sq. SN767344, SA20 0AB,   ☎720393, D2
T2 S4 £26 ('94)
Ash Grove,Llangadog Rd., SN761336, SA20 0DJ, Mrs Theresa Hay, ☎720136,
D1 T1 F1 S1 £12('94)
Erwlon Caravan Park,Brecon Rd, SN779343, Mr.& Mrs.C.R. Rees, ☎720332,
camping and possibility of caravan for 1 night, all facilities.
Tourist Nat. Pk. Information Centre SN766343, ☎720693, bookings.

RHANDIRMWYN, Llandovery,Dyfed.   ☎01550
Youth Hostel, Bryn Poeth Uchaf, SN796439, 22beds - see separate list..
Royal Oak Inn, SN785437, SA20 0NY, ☎760201, D1 T1 F1 S2, £20 ('94)SB
Llanerchindda Farm, Cynghordy, SN807427, SA20 0NB, Nick & Irene Bointon,
☎750274, D4 T4 F1 S1, ES, £19('93) EM£7, Minibus transport provided
for Cambrian Way walkers to and from stages from Brecon Beacons to
Strata Florida, plus mobile phone. See note page 86.
Bwlch-y-Ffin (near Llyn Brianne dam), SN795481, SA20 0PG, Bryan & Pat
Williams, ☎ 760311, D1 T2 £15, EMO.£8 ('95),
Mia'r Nant, SN786436, Mrs Price, ☎760219, D2 T1 F1 £13 ('95).
Nantybai Mill, SN774445, Anthea Jones, ☎ 760211,D2 £12.50('95),teas
1 Nantymwyn Terrace, SN781437,Mrs Jones,☎760202,4 berth caravan
Pen Rhiw Fach, SN782417, Mrs Waddon,☎760234, D1 £13.50('92), 6 berth
caravan (super view), £20.   continued

Camp site (Camping and Caravanning Club), SN779436, ☎ 760257,
Broncwrt, SN769449, Mr.Davis,☎760227,camping nr Towy Bridge Inn
Post Office stores,SN785437, 9am-8pm,7days (summer),last provisions before
Tregaron or Pontrhydfendigaid.`

DOETHIE & UPPER TWYI (TOWY) VALLEYS.
Tyncornel Youth Hostel, SN751534, 18 beds, see separate list.
Dolgoch Youth Hostel, SN806561, 20 beds, see separate list.

TREGARON, Dyfed   ☎01974
Blaencaron Youth Hostel, SN713608, 18 beds, see separate list.
Brynawel, Station Rd., SN679599, SY25 6HX, ☎298310, D1 T1 F2 S1,
    £13.50('94).

PONTRHYDFENDIGAID , Ystrad Meurig, Dyfed.   ☎01974
Llys Teg Guest House, SN731668, SY25 6BB, Mrs Gillian Edwards,
    ☎831697, D2 T1 F1 S3, ES, £18.75, EM £9.75, ('95)
Pantyfedwen,Strata Florida, SY25 6ES, SN755650,Mrs.Davies ☎831358
    D1,T1 F1, £25 inc.EM ('95).
Bronceiro, SN732663, Camping, 831230, showers.

CWMYSTWYTH, Aberystwyth, Dyfed.   ☎0974
Tainewyddion Uchaf, SN791750, Peg & Red Liford, (Wales Wildlife
    Holidays), ☎282672, T3 S1 £8 ('88)
Hafod Lodge, SN784742, SY23 4AD, A.M.Mills, ☎282247, D1 T1 ES,£18,
    transport to EM.
Gelmast, SN777757, Mr Postings, camping,

DEVIL'S BRIDGE, Aberystwyth,Dyfed.   ☎01970
Mount Pleasant, SY23 3LB, SN736769,   Janet & Dave Sherlock,
    ☎890219, D2 T2 S1, £18 ('94) EM £10,
Llysamaeth, SN736770, Mrs Davies, ☎890297, F1 £17.50 ('95).+ flat for 4
Woodlands Camp site, SN746773, Mr Davis, ☎890233 .
Post Office Stores and cafe, SN738769, E & M.Clemas, ☎890228 ECD Sat
    Open Sundays in summer 2-6pm. Sells this guide .

PONTERWYD, Aberystwyth,Dyfed.   ☎01970
Youth Hostel, Ystumtuen, SN735786, 24 beds, see separate list..
Dyffryn Castell Hotel, SN775817, Islwyn & Angharad Jones, ☎890237,
    D2 T1 F5 S1, £17 ('92), SB and restaurant. Transport arranged for
    guests to and from Cambrian Way for stages between
    Ponrhydfendigaid and Commins Coch. See note page 86.
Eisteddfa Gurig Farm, SN798842, Mrs E. Thomas, ☎890684 or 890300
    D2 £14 ('93), EM £5
Post Office stores, SN750808,Mr Shovell, ECD Wed & Sat, Next shop at
    Commins Coch or Mallwyd.
George Borrow Hotel,SN746805,J.Wall, ☎890230.10rooms, £18/20,('95)SB,

DYLIFE, Llanbrynmair,Powys.   ☎01650
Star Inn, SN863940. SY19 7BW, Tony & Susan Banks,☎521345,
    D2 T2 F1S2, £17/18 ('95), SB.
Rhyd-y-Porthmyn, SY19 7BW, SN850939, Patsy & Mike Thompson, ☎521433,
    F2 £18, EMO £10 ('95), Apr-Oct, Indoor heated pool, guided walks.

Maesmedrisiol Farm, Staylittle, SN884945, SY19 7BN, , Mrs Paula Anwyl, ☎521494, D2 T1 F1 S1, £13.50('95), EMO.

LLANBRYNMAIR, & BONT DOLGADFAN , Powys. ☎01650
Cyfeiliog Guest House, Bont Dolgadfan,SY19 7BB, SN886003, Liz & Andrew Fox, ☎521231, D1 T1 F1 £14/15.50, EMO£7.50, ('95),car to and from Way.
Dolgadfan,SN883002, Mrs Anwyl, camping, ☎521245.

COMMINS COCH, Cemmaes, Machynlleth,Powys. ☎01650
Post Office stores, SH844032.
Gwalia, SH853048, SY20 9PU, Harry & Olivia Chandler,☎511377, D1 T1 F1, £14, EM £8 (vegetarian only), ('95), limited camping.
Cefn Goch Uchaf, SH835032, Cemmaes Road, Ian & Eirlys Harris, ☎511552, D2 T1 ES £14 EM £7 ('95), Altitude 221m, panoramic views, path from Darowen road at SH842033, road access from Cemmaes Road.

DINAS MAWDDWY & MALLWYD, Machynlleth, Powys. ☎01650
Buckley Pines Hotel, SH859140, SY20 9LP, Mrs.B.C.Farr, ☎531261, D6 T2 F2 S1, £20-23 ('93), SB, restaurant.
Tremynfa, SH857148, Mrs.O.E.Rees, ☎531240, D2 T1, £10('91).
Gwelafon,SH858146, SY20 9LL,Mrs.E.M.Evans,☎531287,D2 £13.50('94),EMO
Dolbrodmaeth Hotel, SH860137, SY20 9LP, Jean & Graham Williams, ☎531333, D4 T2 F1 S1, self catering unit T + F, B&B £17.50-£22 EM SB, camping, many possibilities.
Red Lion Inn,(Llew Coch), SH859148, Mrs Jenkins, ☎531247, D2,T1 F1, £13.50('92), SB, restaurant. Welsh singing Sat.nights.
Brigands Inn, Mallwyd, SH863125, ☎531208, D3 T4 F2 S2 £16.95(90) restaurant licence
Celyn Brithion camp site, SH861137, L.Rees, ☎531344.
Food shops at Mallwyd and Dinas Mawddwy.

CROSS FOXES, Dolgellau,Gwynedd. ☎01341
Cross Foxes Hotel, SH766167, ☎422487, D2 T1 F1 £16.50/17.50('94) EM SB basic camping

CORRIS, Machynlleth,Powys. ☎01654
Youth Hostel, SH753080, 42 beds, see separate list.
Braich Goch Hotel,SH753075,J&P.Barton,☎761229, D3 T2 S1,.£17('95) EM SB
Bronwydd, Bridge St, SH755077, SY20 9SS, Sue Darbyshire-Robert, ☎761381 D1 T1 F1 S1, £14.50, EMO £7.50, ('95), kitchen available .

MINFFORDD / DOLFFANOG, Talyllyn, Tywyn, Gwynedd. ☎01654
Dolffanog Fach, SH729105, LL36 9AJ, Mrs.Meirwen Pughe, ☎761235, D1,F2, S1, £14-16 ('93), EM £7.50.
Dolffanog Fawr,(next door to above) SH729105 LL36 9AJ, , Pam & Alan Coulter, ☎761247, D2 T1 £18 ('93) EMO. £10.
Dol Einion Camp Site, SH729113, Mrs.M.Rees, T. 0654 761312,showers
Cwmrhwyddfor Farm, Minffordd, SH737120, ☎761286/380, Camp site & B&B.

DOLGELLAU, Gwynedd. ☎01341
Penbryn Croft, Cader Rd.,SH724178, LL40 1RN, Mrs. A. Jones,☎422815 D2 T3 F1,£11 ('91),EMO (6pm)
Tan-y-fron Caravan & Camping Park, SN735176, ☎422638, B&B D1 T1 F1.

Dwy Olwyn, Coed y Fronallt, Llanfachreth Rd, (Cader view), SH734183, Mrs.Norma Jones, ☎422822, D1, T2 F1, £13.50/14.50 ('94), EMO.

ISLAW'R DREF, Dolgellau,Gwynedd.   ☎01341
Kings Youth Hostel, SH683160, 56 beds & camping, see separate list.
Gwernan Lake Hotel, SH704159, ☎422488, D4 T2 S3, £19-25('95) EM
Tyddynmawr, SH703154, Mrs Evans, T.0341 422331, D2 £17 ('94)
Cader Bunkhouse, SH681170 Mr.Rhys ☎423178 or 01248 600478 Sleeps 16, £5 ('93)

ARTHOG, Dolgellau, Gwynedd.   ☎01341
Pen-y-rodyn,SH637141, Mrs Bradbury, ☎250659, D2 T1 £22 EM £10 ('95).
Garthyfog Camp Site, SH636139, small caravan.

BARMOUTH,Gwynedd.   ☎01341
Bay View, 6 Porkington Terrace LL42 1LY, SH619156, Colin & Vera Portman, T.0341 280284, D1 T2 F1 £12.50 ('93).EMO.
Bryn Melyn Hotel, Panorama Rd, LL42 1DQ, SH620158, Carol & David Clay, ☎280556/280990, D5 T2 F1 ES £19.50-£27, EM, Transport arranged to/from Way between Commins Coch and Cwm Bychan, see note page 86
Lawrenny Lodge Hotel, SH620156, LL42 1DQ, Mr.&Mrs K.Barber,☎280466 about 10 rooms, £15-21('94),restaurant.
Several others, notably on Marine Parade, SH610159,

CWM NANTCOL, Llanbedr,Gwynedd.   ☎01341
Craig Isaf, SH635259, Mr Jones, ☎241341,camping.

LLANBEDR, Gwynedd.   ☎01341
Youth Hostel, SH585267, 47 beds, see separate list.
Glanwern, SH584270,LL45 2HL, M.& R. Fuller, ☎241292, D1 T1 F1 S1 £12,EMF£4 ('95)
The Mill, SH589268, Mrs Roberts, camp site,caravans to let.

CWM BYCHAN, Llanbedr,Gwynedd.
Camping, SH646315, no toilets.

HARLECH, Gwynedd.   ☎01766
Byrdir Hotel, High St, SH582310, LL46 2YA, Pat & Ken Elford. ☎780316, TD12 S3 £13.50-£15.50 ('94) EM
Queens Hotel, Morfa Rd, SH581315, LL46 2YA,Clare & Dave Birch, ☎780480, D2 T4, £15 ('93), SB EM £5.50.
Castle Cottage Hotel, SH582313, ☎780479, D2 F2, ES £17-25 ('94) EM
TAXI service (e.g. to and from Cwm Bychan and Cwm Nantcol), M.G.Parry, Tan-yr-allt, (opp station), ☎780392.

TRAWSFYNYDD,Gwynedd.   ☎01766
Trawsfynydd Holiday Village, Bronaber, SH716319, 280 Norwegian style log cabins, 4, 6 & 8 berth, ☎540219/374, app £40 cabin.

FFESTINIOG, Blaenau Ffestiniog,Gwynedd.   ☎01766
Moranedd Guest House, SH704423, LL41 4LGG, G.& R. Lethbridge, ☎762734, D2 T2F1 S1, £16-18 ('95)

GELLILYDAN / MAENTWROG, Blaenau Ffestiniog, Gwynedd.　　　☎01766
   Gwynfryn, Gellilydan,SH685398, LL41 4EE, Mrs.G.Jones,　☎590225,
      D1 F1 S1 £12.50('95)
   Bryn Arms,Gellilydan SH688396, SB
   Llwyn Farm, Gellilydan, SH683392,camping
   Post Office, Bron-y-wern, Maentwrog, SH665405, LL41 4HN, , Mrs.E.Jackson,
      ☎590210, D1 T1 S1, £12 ('94)
   Grapes Hotel, SH665406, LL41 4HN, ☎590208, D3 S3, £25, Restaurant.
   Plas Tan-y-Bwlch, (Snowdonia National Park Study Centre), SH655406,
      ☎590324, Dinner B&B £27 ('93), Availability dependant on courses.
   Llechrwd camp site, SH678413, Mrs Edwards. showers.

BEDDGELERT Gwynedd.　　　☎01766
   Plas Colwyn, SH589482, LL55 4UY, John & Lynda Osmond, ☎890458, D2 T1
      F2 S1 £15-19('95), EM restaurant, Transport　for guests to and from
      Cambrian Way for stages between Cwm Bychan and Conwy,see page 86
   Mizpah, Plas Tan-y-craig, SH591482, LL55 4LT, Brian & Gwen Maddison,
      ☎890329, F6, Fr £15,('95) EM £8
   Colwyn, SH589482, Mrs.J. Williams, LL55 4UY,☎890276, S2 D2 T1 F1 £17(95)

NANT GWYNANT, Caernarfon, Gwynedd.　　　☎01766
   Bryn Gwynant Youth Hostel, 70 beds, SH641513. See separate list.
   Glan Gwynant Country Guest House, SH639514, Mr.& Mrs.K.Harper, ☎890440
      ,D2 T2 F1 £16(94), EM £10.
   Bryn Dinas, LL55 4NH, SH625503, Jerry & Barbara Rogers, ☎890234.
      Bunk beds for 23 in house £7.25 ('95), accom for 26 in timber cabins £5.95.
      Own sleeping bags and pillow cases essential. Kitchen in house,also in
      separate bunkhouse. Meals can be provided. Booking essential.

PEN-Y-PASS & PEN-Y-GWRYD, Nant Gwynant, Gwynedd.　　　☎01286
   Pen-y-Pass Youth Hostel, 117 beds, SH647556, see separate list.
   Pen-y-Gwryd Hotel, SH660558, LL55 4NT, Briggs/Pullee, ☎870211 & 870768,
      £19-£23 ('93),dinner £12, Breakfast 9am.

OGWEN , Bethesda, Gwynedd..
   Idwal Cottage Youth Hostel, SH648603, 56 beds,see separate list.
   Gwern Gof Uchaf, camp site　SH673603,
   Gwern Gof Isaf camp site, SH685601.D& E Williams, ☎01690 720276
      bunkhouse for 6 (Williams Barn), £2.50 ('93).

CAPEL CURIG, Betws-y-Coed, Gwynedd.　　　☎01690
   Youth Hostel, SH726579, 60 beds, see separate list.

ROEWEN, Conwy,Gwynedd.　　　☎01492
   Youth Hostel, 27 beds, self catering, SH747721, see separate list.

CONWY, Gwynedd.　　　☎01492
   15 Cadnant Park, SH776777, LL32 8PR, Mrs.N.M.Hughes, ☎592319, D2 T1 F2
      £13.50 ('95)
   Also 13,& 25 Cadnant Park and Llys Gwilym,3 Mountain Rd off Cadnant Park.
   Bryn Corach, HF Holidays Ltd, Sychnant Pass Rd, SH775774, 84 beds. Bookings
      ☎0181 905 9558 or at short notice ☎01492 596339
   Colwyn Bay Youth Hostel, SH847776, 87 beds, see separate list.

GLOSSARY OF WELSH WORDS AND PLACE NAMES
ON THE CAMBRIAN WAY

ABER   rivermouth
ADAR   bird
AFON   river
AGEN ALLWEDD   keyhole cave
ALLT   wooded hill
BACH   & FACH   small
BEDDGELERT   grave of Gelert
BLAEN valley head
BRYN   hill
BUGEILYN   sheep pasture
BWLCH   mountain pass
CADAIR IDRIS   ldris's chair
CAER   fort
CAPEL-Y-FFIN   chapel on the border
CASEG   mare
CASTELL   castle
CARN & GARN   cairn, heap of stones
CARNEDDAU cairns
CEMAIS   bend in river
CNEWR   meandering stream
CNICHT   knight
COCH   red
COED   wood
COMMINS COCH   red commons
CRAIG   crag cliff
CROCBEN   gallows
DAU & DWY   two
DDU & DU   two
DDUALLT   black hillside
DIAL GARREG   stone of revenge
DIFFWYS   wilderness,precipice
DINAS   hill,fortress
DOLGELLAU   meadow of the monks'-
DOMEN & TOMEN   mound cells
DRUM   ridge
DRWS   narrow pass
DWYRYD   two fords or streams
DWYGYFYLCHI   two round forts
DYFFRYN CASTELL valley of the river
DYLIFE   floods   Castell
EGLWYS   church
ESGAIR   ridge
FAEN   stone
FAN   peak
FAWR & MAWR   large
FFORDD   ford
FOEL & MOEL   bare hill
GABALFA   ferry
GALLT   slope
GARN GRON   round cairn
GELLI   grove
GLAN   riverbank
GLAS   blue/green
HAFOD   summer dwelling
HARLECH   beautiful rock
HENDRE   winter dwelling
IS   below
ISAF   lower
LIBANUS   Lebanon
LLAN   church
LLANDDEUSANT church of two saints
LLETHYR   slope
LLUEST TY MAWR   hill farm of big -
LLWYN-Y-CELYN   holly grove. house
LLWYN ONN   ash grove

LLYN   lake
LLYWERNOG   place of foxes
MAES   meadow
MAESTEG   fair meadow
MAEN   stone
MAENTWROG   stone of Twrog
MALLWYD   grey field
MINFFORDD   edge of road
MOEL,MOELFRE   bare hill
MYDDFAI   meadow of the round
MYNYDD   mountain   hollow
NANT   brook
NEWYDD   new
NEUADD   mansion
EOR   cold
OGOF   cave
OLEU   light
PANT   hollow
PANTYFEDWEN hollow of birch
PEN   peak or top.   trees
PENMAENMAWR head of large rock
PENNANT   head of stream or valley
PENGENFFORDD   head of ridge road
PEN-Y-FAN   top of the peak
PENYGWRYD-GWRYD   length of
                      outstretched arm
PLAS   mansion
PUMLUMON (Plynlimon)   five peaks
POETH   hot
PONT & BONT   bridge
PONTERWYD   bridge of poles
PONTARFRYNACH bridge over the
river MYNACH(monk),(Devils Bridge)
PONTRHYDFENDIGAID   bridge of
the blessed ones
PONTSTICILL   bridge of the stile
PWLL   pit, pool
PYSGOTWR fishermen
RHANDIRMWYN   land of minerals
RHIW   hillside
RHOS   moorland
RHYD   ford
RO-WEN   white pebbles
SARN   paved way
SCWD   waterfall
SYCHNANT   stream that dries up
TAL   end
TALWRN   rocky place
TALYLLYN   end of the lake
TORPANTAU   break in the hollows
TRAWSFYNYDD   across the m'tain
TRYFAN   high pointed mountain
TWYMYN   feverish
TY   house
TY BACH   little house (toilet)
TYNCORNEL   house in the corner
WAUN   moorland , meadow
WAUN OER   cold moorland
WEN   white
YSTRAD   wide valley bottom
YSTRADFELLTE   valley of the
                      MELLTE(swift)
YSGYFARNOGOD bare hill of hares
YR WYDDFA(Snowdon summit)
                      grave

THE CHECK POINTS

To have walked the Cambrian Way route described in this guidebook it is not necessary to follow the exact route prescribed, in fact individuality is to be encouraged, provided it does not involve trespass. However, to give some yardstick of achievement the following check points must have been visited on a continuous walk, though the walk need not necessarily have been on consecutive days.

1	ST	180765	Cardiff Castle	22	SH	833136	Bwlch Siglen
2	ST	131827	Castell Coch	23	SH	711130	Cader Idris
3	ST	224900	Mynydd Machen	24	SH	620155	Barmouth Bridge
4	ST	242926	Twmbarlwm	25	SH	661258	Y Llethyr
5	SO	270119	Blorenge	26	SH	665270	Rhinog Fach
6	SO	272188	Sugar Loaf	27	SH	657290	Rhinog Fawr
7	SO	255315	Capel-y-ffin	28	SH	659347	Moel Ysgyfarnogod
8	SO	225351	Tumpa	29	SH	683359	Moelfryn
9	SO	216290	Waun Fach	30	SH	658449	Moelwyn Mawr
10	SO	207243	Pen Allt Mawr	31	SH	648467	Cnicht
11	SO	192157	Eglwys Faen	32a	SH	594462	Pont Aberglaslyn or
12	SO	012216	Pen-y-fan	32b	SH	641513	Bryn Gwynant YH
13a	SN	881191	Fan Gihirych or	33	SH	610544	Snowdon
13b	SN	408144	Blaen Nedd Isaf.junc	34	SH	643579	Glyder Fawr
14	SN	825218	Bannau Brycheiniog	35	SH	656583	Glyder Fach
15	SN	767447	Towy Bridge	36	SH	666608	Tal-y-llyn Ogwen
16	SN	740610	Garn Gron	37	SH	663631	Carnedd Dafydd
17	SN	809720	Doman Milwyn	38	SH	684645	Carnedd Llewelyn
18	SN	727782	Pontbren Plwca	39	SH	729727	Tal-y-fan
19	SN	790869	Plynlimon	40	SH	760778	Conwy Mountain
20	SN	861940	Dylife	41	SH	783775	Conwy Castle
21	SH	859149	Dinas Mawddwy				

USEFUL ADDRESSES

Ramblers Association. Central Office, 1/5 Wandsworth Rd., London SW8 2XX, 0171 582 6878. For membership details and postal sales of this book.
Welsh Office, Tŷ'r Cerddwyr, High St, Gresford, Wrexham, Clwyd LL12 8PT, 01978 855148.

Offa's Dyke Association. Old Primary School, West St., Knighton, Powys, LD7 IEN, 01547 528753. Send s.a.e. for information on Offa's Dyke Path, Glyndwr's Way, and postal sales of this book.

Snowdonia National Park . Penrhyndeudraeth, Gwynedd, LL48 6LS, 01766 770274.

Snowdonia National Park Society. Ty Hyll (The Ugly House) (SH 757575), Capel Curig, Betws-y-coed, Gwynedd, LL24 ODS, 01690 720287.

Brecon Beacons National Park, 7 Glamorgan St. Brecon, LD3 7DP. 01874 624437

Brecon Beacons Park Society, Tyn-y-Bryn, Deriside, Abergavenny, Gwent, NP7 7HT 01873 856682

Campaign for the Protection of Rural Wales Tŷ Gwyn , 31 High St ., Welshpool, Powys, SY21 7JP, 01938 552525

Long Distance Walkers Association, Sec.B. Smith, 10 Temple Park Close, Leeds, W.Yorks, LS15 0JJ, 01532 642205.

British Upland Footpath Trust, PO Box 96,Manchester M20 2FU,01204 529905

ABBREVIATIONS

B&B	bed and breakfast	NT	National Trust
bdy	boundary	OS	Ordnance Survey
BG	bridle gate	otw	old tramway
Br	bracken	P	car park
Bn	barn	p	limited parking
BTCV	British Trust for Conservation Volunteers	pa	path-
Ca	cairn	PC	public convenience, toilets
ECD	early closing day(shops)	PH	public house,inn,pub
En	enclosed	PO	post office and shop
ES	En Suite,i.e. private toilet & bath and/or shower	RA	Ramblers Association
		Qu	quarry
F	fence	Rd	road
FB	footbridge	Res	reservoir
F&C	fish and chips	Rp	road used as public path
FC	Forestry Commission	RSPB	Royal Society for the Protection of Birds
FE	Forest Enterprise(FC)		
FG	fieldgate	Ru	ruined building
Fm	farm	Sh	shop selling food
FmRd	farm road	Sn	stone
FoRd	forest road	SP	signpost
GL	green lane	Sta	railway station
HG	hunting gate (about metre wide)	Tr	track
		T	telephone call box
i	information /tourist office	Und	undefined route
ind	indistinct route	Urd	untarred road
int	intermittent path	Wm	waymarked path
KG	kissing gate	YHA	Youth Hostels Association
LS	double ladder stile	YH	Youth Hostel
MeF	square mesh fence		

KEY TO STRIP MAPS

Recommended Cambrian Way route, including Hostel and major variants

on paths or undefined   on roads

Roads   major   minor

Selected other paths and side routes

Railways and stations   buildings

Field boundaries, where shown   camp sites

Rivers   streams   lakes, sea

Boundaries of inset maps on 1: 50, 000 maps

Trees   deciduous   coniferous   Youth Hostels

Summits   ▲   churches, chapels   +

Scales - maps with numbers only - 1: 50,000 (including 17A)

    maps with numbers and letters - 1:25,000 unless otherwise stated

North is at the top of the maps unless otherwise stated

Mileage points   —O   Electric power lines